FORCES OF NATURE

FORCES OF NATURE

By the Editors of Time-Life Books

TIME-LIFE BOOKS, ALEXANDRIA, VIRGINIA

CONTENTS

RESHAPING THE EARTH

The surface of the earth is usually a source of calm and comfort. Storm-tossed seafarers and aviators long for the feel of firm ground beneath their feet; strong and reliable people are described as solid as a rock. At times, however, the earth presents an unpredictably fearsome face: Once-solid ground turns liquid; the earth gapes wide and swallows streets and buildings.

When the forces of nature are quiet again, the face of the earth has been altered. Mountains have been moved, rivers relocated, and strange figures inscribed on the land. But even when the earth seems to sleep, it continues to change and reshape itself. With millions of years at its disposal, nature has worked some wonders: Great glassy balls have been deposited on wooded hills, and forms resembling religious icons crystallize within the earth. Whirling waters laced with sand and stone carve the hardest granite, minerals silently cement together whimsical structures one grain at a time, and stones seem somehow to slither unaided across parched lands.

Scientists have managed to describe some of these marvels, but many details remain elusive. Maps and measurements can show how pieces of the earth's crust move and grind against each other like floes of ice, sending tremors throughout the globe. But they cannot tell where or when the next quakes will rearrange the earth. Nor can they fully explain such things as ghostly roars that sometimes boom from desert sands, or musical rocks, or slabs of stone that sag from their own weight.

1

Earthquake Weather

On October 17, 1989, Margaret Owings noticed that the California air seemed strangely still and sultry. "Earthquake weather," thought the longtime resident of Big Sur, about 100 miles south of San Francisco. And sure enough, that evening as millions of Americans prepared to watch the third game of the World Series on television, they instead saw northern California shaken by the destructive Loma Prieta earthquake.

Like Margaret Owings, natives of earthquake-prone regions have long insisted that they can sense imminent tremors from such clues as unusual animal behavior, chemical changes in well water, strange lights, groaning noises from the earth, or the ominous calm of so-called earthquake weather.

Until recently, scientists have claimed that the folklore was without foundation. Yet today, as researchers employ increasingly sophisticated equipment and record ever-more-subtle earthquake-related phenomena, they are becoming more respectful of tradition—and finding within it manifestations of a complex web of events surrounding an earthquake.

For example, some researchers now speculate that "earthquake weather" may be real, after all. The squeezing of the earth just before a quake, they posit, generates electric currents that break down trapped ground water and release hydrogen and oxygen ions into the atmosphere. The ions, it is said, may produce fog, clouds, and the peculiar calm associated with earthquake weather. The same electric charges may also be responsible for "earthquake lights," the fireballs, flashes, or eerie glow in the sky reported before or during a tremor. □

In this rare photograph, an eerie, bluish glow appears on the horizon moments before a 1966 earthquake in the town of Matsushiro, Japan.

New World Atlantis

The long-held belief that earthquakes were the work of a wrathful God received terrifying reinforcement on June 7, 1692, when three tremors shook Jamaica so violently that two mountains were moved nearly a mile from their original positions. Damage was greatest in the notorious British colonial city of Port Royal, a New World Gomorrah that had served for forty-five years as a center of the West Indian rum and slave trade.

Built on an unstable spit of land, Port Royal abruptly slid into the ocean when the quake struck; within minutes, much of it lay under fifty feet of water. Nearly two thousand people—one-third of the population—perished.

Many of those who escaped seemed to survive only by divine favor. The frigate *Swan*, lying in a slipway on the east side of town, was sent skimming into the drowning city atop a huge wave. Her dangling ropes offered providential lifelines; those who grabbed them were carried to safety when the ship grounded atop a sunken building. Merchant Lewis Galdy, swallowed alive by a fissure that opened beneath his feet when the second shock struck, was shot safely out like a popped cork by the force of the third tremor.

But hundreds more were entombed in the deep cracks, and their rotting corpses sent up a noxious odor that hung over the island for months. Rapidly covered by layers of silt, the submerged portion of the town lay forgotten and virtually intact until it was excavated in 1959. □

Lisbon's Unholy Survivors

The cathedral and churches of Lisbon were packed with worshipers on All Saints' Day in 1755. The holy day mass had just begun when suddenly the buildings swayed like storm-tossed vessels and then crashed down in ruins *(above)*. Throughout the city, the great stone palaces of merchants and nobles collapsed. Within two minutes, 30,000 of Lisbon's population of 275,000 were crushed to death. Another 20,000 residents—perhaps many more—perished in the fires that quickly broke out in the city or drowned in fifty-foot ocean waves, called tsunamis, that swept into the port.

The tremors radiated over an area of 1.5 million square miles and were felt by one-third of Europe's population. Rivers as far away as Scandinavia and Scotland surged wildly. A thousand miles north of Lisbon, in Luxembourg, an army barracks fell, killing 500 soldiers; to the south, 10,000 Moroccans died in the tremors and the resulting tsunamis.

In destroying one of Europe's richest and most notably devout capitals, the Lisbon earthquake has been credited with cracking the foundations of prevailing philosophical assumptions, principally the belief in a just and harmoniously ordered universe. And nature's challenge seemed to be issued with a mocking smirk: At the same time that most of the city's churches were utterly destroyed, its brothels emerged unscathed. □

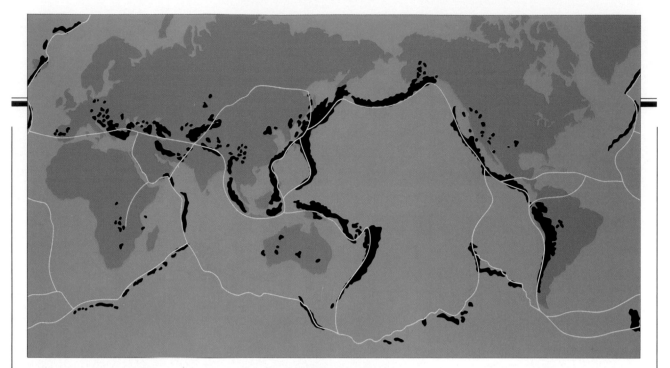

The Puzzle of Rogue Quakes

Riding down a Kentucky road in December 1811, naturalist John James Audubon saw what he took to be a tornado approaching over the western horizon. He spurred his horse on, hoping to outrun the storm. But instead of leaping forward, the animal slowed to a cautious walk, then halted and spread out all four legs as if to brace itself. "At that instant all the shrubs and trees began to move from their very roots, the ground rose and fell in successive furrows, like the ruffled waters of a lake," Audubon wrote. "The earth waved like a field of corn before the breeze."

The unexpected sensation was the opening salvo of an awesome series of earthquakes. Over the following three months, three quakes centered in New Madrid, Missouri, flattened hundreds of square miles of forests, altered the course of the Mississippi River, turned thousands of acres of prairie into swamp, and destroyed the town of New Madrid itself—actually lowering the ground beneath it a full fifteen feet.

The final and most destructive tremor, on February 7, 1812, was felt over an area of 1.5 million square miles—one-half the size of the present-day continental United States. It rattled windows in Washington and rang church bells in Boston, Massachusetts and Charleston, South Carolina.

Seventy-four years later, Charleston would reply, after a fashion. On August 31, 1886, the city was severely damaged by an earthquake that nearly equaled the intensity of the New Madrid quake. It would be felt as far west as Omaha.

In addition to their devastating force, the New Madrid and Charleston quakes had in common extraordinary locations. According to scientific understanding both past and present, they should not have occurred where they did. Although the causes of earthquakes were little understood in the nineteenth century, it was known—and had been known since the days of ancient Greece—that tremors could be expected in some locations quite frequently and in others

hardly ever. Charleston and New Madrid fell into the latter category.

In the midtwentieth century, the earth sciences were revolutionized by a powerful theory known as plate tectonics, which accounted for most earthquakes. According to the theory, the surface of the earth is composed of six major plates—and at least nine smaller ones—that float atop a mantle of molten rock. The plates are constantly in motion—grinding together, drifting apart, and even sliding over one another. Ninety-five percent of all earthquakes occur where two plates meet.

The theory leaves unexplained both the New Madrid and Charleston quakes, which took place in the interior of a continental plate. But researchers may have found the cause of the Missouri tremors—friction between the fluid mantle and a previously undetected fault, or crack, in the moving continental plate. As for the Charleston quake, some scientists suspect a so-called pluton, a dense mass of solidified molten rock that welled into the earth's crust, where it can create violent stresses. □

Earthquakes strike most frequently in the regions marked in black on the map at the top of the page. Ninety-five percent fall along the boundaries of continental plates (outlined in orange).

The Death of Old San Francisco

On April 20, 1906, actor John Barrymore sat down to write an eyewitness account of the devastating earthquake that had struck San Francisco two days earlier. "What I had seen in those harrowing days and what I myself had been through—people shot on the streets, spiked on bayonets and other horrors so great that the imagination was almost blunt from contemplating them," the great Shakespearean scribbled with dramatic embellishment.

In truth, Barrymore—who had been romancing another man's fiancée when the quake struck and drinking steadily ever since—made the whole thing up. Yet his drunken ramblings, which he hoped to peddle to a New York magazine, were not far off the mark. The destruction of San Francisco truly beggared the imagination.

Two fierce tremors shook northern California just after 5:00 a.m. on April 18. The shocks toppled sea cliffs, felled 500-year-old redwoods, and, at Stanford University, pitched a statue of nineteenth century geologist Louis Agassiz headfirst into a sidewalk *(left)*. Roads, fences, streams, and other features were severed and displaced by as much as fifteen feet along a 200-mile stretch of the San Andreas Fault, whose movement was responsible for the tremors.

But the quake's most horrible effects were felt in San Francisco, where thousands of buildings were destroyed and more than 700 people killed. Explosive fires fueled by ruptured gas mains raged out of control for three days, lighting up scenes of mass horror and individual tragedy. ◊

Whole families died in the wreckage of timber houses built on unstable landfill around San Francisco Bay. One man, fleeing the ruins of the house where his wife had been crushed to death, thrust his two infant children into suitcases to carry them to safety; when he opened the cases later, both children had suffocated.

Meanwhile, drunken looters roasted chunks of sausage over the glowing coals of the burning city, and prostitutes plied their trade in tents along the edges of the ruins.

Amid the dreadful chaos came one astonishing grace note. Dazed guests standing half-dressed on the sidewalk outside the tottering Palace Hotel suddenly heard the sound of Enrico Caruso's magnificent tenor welling up over the clamor. To calm the famous Italian opera star, who had been in San Francisco to perform in the opera *Carmen*, his conductor had ordered him to sing.

Perhaps the strangest sights of all were to be found in Chinatown *(below)*—a warren of rickety buildings built over a subterranean network of opium dens and bordellos. The fire swept the area clean. Hundreds of terrified residents fled the conflagration, and at their heels swarmed thousands of squealing rats—some infected with bubonic plague, a fact that was hushed up by local authorities. Over the next year, more than 150 cases of the plague struck the ruined city.

When the fires were finally brought under control, they had consumed 520 city blocks and 28,188 buildings. Damages were estimated at $500 million; many insurance companies were bankrupted by subsequent claims.

The city was financially gutted as well, most of its banks incinerated along with the currency inside their vaults. Yet one member of the financial community remained in business. Amadeo Peter Giannini, president of the tiny Bank of Italy, had fled the fire with his institution's entire capital of $80,000 in sacks guarded by rifle-toting relatives. As soon as the fires were out, Giannini set a plank

across two empty barrels and began loaning money to those who wanted to rebuild San Francisco.

Giannini's little stall eventually grew into the mighty Bank of America, and a rebuilt San Francisco once again assumed its place among the great cities of America. For those who had lived there before the great quake, however, the golden city by the bay—gaudy, exotic, imbued with a heady sense of its gold rush heritage—would never be the same. "The old San Francisco is dead," mourned one longtime resident. "It is as though a pretty, frivolous woman had passed through a great tragedy. She survives, but she is sobered and different." □

Trembling earth returned to San Francisco during the evening rush hour on October 17, 1989, when an earthquake rocked northern California, killing 100 people and injuring 3,000. Although damage was heavy in Oakland and other area cities, the earthquake's effect on the city of San Francisco was confined to isolated areas such as the Marina district, where wooden apartment buildings constructed on unstable filled land collapsed and burned (above).

An Italian City of the Dead

"The spectacle that greets the eye here is beyond the imagination of Jules Verne," wrote an appalled rescuer upon viewing the Sicilian seaport of Messina three days after Christmas, 1908, when it was obliterated by an earthquake. Then the eighth largest port in Italy—and a magnet for tourists—Messina was shaken like a rag for more than thirty seconds by two major shocks and a series of erratic undulations. In those brief, horrifying moments, the entire city crashed to the earth, its citizens caught by the tens of thousands in a wild jumble of mortar, bricks, chimneys, roofs, and walls. The few structures that survived soon received a deadly one-two punch: Water released by broken dams flooded down from above, and a tsunami rushed in from the sea.

Horror followed upon unrelenting horror. Eighty-six thousand dead were crushed in the rubble or drowned in the harbor. A man who raced into his ruined house to rescue his infant son found the child missing and his bed full of fish. Thousands more of the living were trapped in the ruins for days, waving their arms and legs in a vain attempt to attract help. "Several died gnawing their arms and hands, evidently delirious from pain and hunger," wrote one witness to the macabre scene. "One woman's teeth were firmly fixed in the leg of a dead babe," he wrote.

Only 5,000 people escaped death, entrapment, or crippling

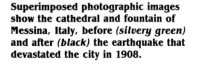

Superimposed photographic images show the cathedral and fountain of Messina, Italy, before *(silvery green)* and after *(black)* the earthquake that devastated the city in 1908.

injury. They could only wander the ruins and avoid the 750 convicts who were set loose by the destruction of nearby Cappuccini Prison. Reeling drunkenly through the city, the escaped prisoners hacked jewelry from dead fingers and throats; one group careened into a fashionable dress shop and emerged crazily dressed in the latest Paris creations. By noon that day, carrion birds were greedily plucking at the dead; at nightfall they were joined by wild dogs and rats. That night, the once-lovely seaport acquired the nickname Citta di Morte, "City of the Dead."

Engineers who studied the ruins later blamed Messina's architects and builders for much of the death and destruction. Most of the town's imposing buildings were carelessly built of river stones, brick, and sandy mortar, and covered by impressive-looking but fragile stone facades. Only one house was left intact. It had been built of reinforced concrete and iron at the direction of a merchant who was derided as an eccentric. □

An earthquake on August 17, 1959, tilted the shores of Montana's Hebgen Lake like a giant bowl, submerging cabins at one end and lifting docks high and dry at the other.

Earth Waves

For centuries, survivors of earthquakes have reported seeing the earth undulate like the ocean's surface shortly after the quake's tremors ceased.

Scientists discounted such reports until the 1980s, when seismologist Rene Rodriguez worked out a theoretical explanation: If an elastic upper layer of earth, such as clay, covers a more rigid lower layer, the more elastic layer may indeed ripple independently when the two are shaken. □

Liquid Land

An apartment building in Niigata, Japan, lies on its back after an earthquake in 1967, a victim of "soil liquefaction." Seemingly solid earth turns into a viscous liquid when wet, sandy soil is vibrated; the sand particles float apart, turning into a soupy quicksand with the consistency of porridge.

During the 1967 quake, residents sank in the liquid earth. No drownings were reported, however, because the quicksandlike soil permitted people to float. Twenty-six did die when the tremors leveled three thousand homes. □

Alaska's Bad Good Friday

On Good Friday, March 27, 1964, the south central coast of Alaska was rocked by the most violent earthquake to hit North America in the twentieth century. Radiating from its epicenter along the shores of Prince William Sound, eighty miles southeast of Anchorage, the tremors shook Alaska for an astounding seven minutes. (Most quakes last merely seconds.)

As if struck by a giant clapper, the earth rang like a bell. (It would continue to vibrate for three weeks.) More than 100,000 square miles of the earth's surface were heaved up or dropped downward— the largest land area deformed by a single earthquake in historic times. Huge tsunamis spread outward across the Pacific, sweeping the beaches of Hawaii, Japan, and the west coast of the United States. Shock waves radiating through the North American continent lifted the ground beneath the city of Houston, Texas, and Cape Kennedy, Florida.

Despite the magnitude of the quake, relatively few lives were lost, thanks to the sparse population of Alaska and a fortunate fluke of timing. In hard-hit Anchorage, the two elementary schools and the high school were all empty when they collapsed, and the Denali movie theater *(below)* slipped into a fissure moments before it was to open its doors for the first show of the day.

But the property damage cost Alaskans some $500 million. Undaunted, they quickly began rebuilding—sometimes displaying a gritty humor about the disaster. One Anchorage businessman, whose office building had fallen into a giant crack, nailed up over the wreckage a sign bearing the wry message: "I knew it would be tough to make a living in Alaska, but I never thought I'd go this far in the hole." □

Earthquake? Ask a Snake

In Japan and China, fish, pheasants, and other animals have long been valued for their ability to sense impending earthquakes. In Turkey, the appearance of bats during the day is said to signal a coming quake. And residents of the Soviet Union's Kamchatka Peninsula brace for shocks when the normally sluggish native bears begin to act spritely.

For more than two millennia, animals have been watched for signs of earthquake behavior:

• Five days before the 373 BC earthquake that leveled Helas, Greece, rats, snakes, weasels, centipedes, worms, and beetles migrated out of the city in droves.

• Dogs in Messina, Italy, howled so uncontrollably before an earthquake in 1783 that they could be silenced only by being shot.

• The night before an earthquake struck the city of Naples in 1805, swarms of locusts were seen creeping through the streets in the direction of the sea.

• Eels crowded onto the beach in Sanriku, Japan, in advance of an earthquake and tsunami in 1896.

• Two minutes before a 1910 quake in Landsberg, Germany, all of the city's bees flew from their hives in a storm of excitement, returning only after the shocks passed.

• The day of the great Alaskan earthquake of 1964 *(page 16)*, giant Kodiak bears came out of hibernation two weeks ahead of time, leaving their rocky caves on a run.

• An hour before a 1966 quake, startled residents of Tashkent, in the Soviet Republic of Uzbekistan, watched a mass migration of ants carrying their eggs.

• Two hours in advance of a 1969 quake, authorities in Tientsin, China, issued a warning based on the agitated behavior of the zoo's Manchurian tigers, giant pandas, yaks, deer, and other animals.

• In February 1975, two days before a great quake struck Haicheng, China, pigs fought frantically in their sties, some biting off other pigs' tails. Hours before the tremors started, hibernating snakes left their burrows and froze to death rather than return to the earth. □

Scalding Mud

A devastating series of earthquakes that struck western Calabria, at the tip of Italy's toe, for two months in 1783 began with a massive tremor that ripped countless fissures in the earth—some as wide as 150 feet—and tapped deep springs of boiling water. Hundreds of animals and humans fell into the crevices, only to be spit violently back out on scalding geysers of gaseous mud. Those who survived the ordeal were crippled for life by their burns. Ultimately, more than 30,000 died in the quakes. □

L.A. Debris Flow

Awakened by a crash of thunder one stormy February night in 1978, Jackie Genofile of Los Angeles and her two children stood transfixed at a window of their home in the foothills of the San Gabriel Mountains. As Mrs. Genofile later described the sight: "It was just one big black thing coming at us, rolling, rolling with a lot of water in front of it, pushing the water, this big black thing."

The "thing" was a debris flow—a viscous soup of water, soil, rocks, and boulders with the consistency of freshly mixed concrete—that slammed into the Genofile home moments later. It deposited thirteen automobiles around the house, including five in the swimming pool, and left a twelve-foot-high drift of muddy rubble in the front yard. The mass poured through the windows and doors and filled the interior within six minutes, but it miraculously spared the Genofiles themselves, who found a few inches of breathing space below the ceiling of the master bedroom.

Debris flows are a common phenomenon on the slopes of the San Gabriels, a range of mountains stretching eastward along the edge of heavily populated metropolitan Los Angeles. In geological terms, they are among the world's newest—and therefore most unstable—mountain ranges, still heaving upward while simultaneously shedding pieces of their rocky hide. The mountains' molting is abetted by the winter rains, which provide the water to lubricate the unstable earth and send it down the slopes and into houses all along the San Gabriel front.

A rock-filled car *(top photo)* rests by the rooftop of a buried house, where it was swept by tons of rock and mud from the San Gabriels. Huge catch basins *(lower photo)* cannot contain the debris flows.

In the hope of catching the debris before it can do any damage, local authorities have dug 120 football-field-size pits high on the hillsides; concrete pillars are set above the pits to stop the largest rocks. But the rampaging earth frequently overwhelms these man-made defenses and slithers down streets and through houses, sometimes rolling boulders right into the communities that spread across the valley floor.

One such town is Pasadena, home of the Rose Bowl. Above the stadium, a reservoir built to hold water is now brimming with San Gabriel Mountain sand and gravel. A contractor excavates the debris and sells it for construction—and the mountains fill the reservoir as quickly as he can dig. □

Armero's Muddy Death

The 1985 eruption of Colombia's long-dormant volcano Nevado del Ruiz killed some 20,000 people in a uniquely ghastly manner—not by hot steam, ash, or lava, but in a suffocating sea of gluey mud.

As residents of the fertile lower slopes slept on the night of November 20, two detonations shot millions of tons of ash into the cool Andean air. Ramón Antonio Rodriguez, mayor of the town of Armero, was at his ham radio, calmly describing the event to a fellow ham operator in Ibaque, sixty miles away, when he suddenly shouted: "Wait a minute! I think the town is getting flooded." Then the radio went dead. At that instant, the prosperous agricultural community of 22,500 was engulfed in a mile-wide river of cold slime. Rodriguez and most of his fellow townspeople were trapped and killed; four out of five buildings in Armero were buried, leaving what one survivor later described as "one big beach of mud."

The sticky substance covering Armero was a mixture of volcanic debris and icy water produced when hot magma inside the volcano melted the mountain's snow-cap. The viscous, chilled fluid swept at speeds up to thirty miles per hour down the side of the mountain. As it raced through Armero, thousands of people were instantly entombed in up to fifteen feet of muck.

As the torrent rushed on, it warmed and grew into a steaming river as much as fifty feet deep, and the destruction at Armero was repeated in other communities nearby. For days after the eruption, rescuers still struggled to extricate trapped survivors—many unable to shout for help because their mouths were plugged by the mud.

Ironically, the volcano had been belching up occasional columns of smoke for more than a year, and a Colombian government agency had predicted the disaster almost two months before it struck. But authorities had been taking their time in responding to the warnings. As Darrel Herd, an expert on volcanoes and earthquakes at the U.S. Geological Survey, put it: "The volcano erupted too soon." □

The faint outlines of ruined buildings are all that remain of four-fifths of Armero, Colombia, after a mile-wide river of icy mud swept through, triggered by the eruption of a nearby volcano, Nevado del Ruiz.

Pennsylvania Pothole

In 1884, coal miners working forty-five feet below ground in Archbald, Pennsylvania, set off a dynamite blast to loosen a seam of coal. But when the men returned to the mine after the explosion, they found that they had uncovered not only coal but also a huge, circular stone chamber containing large quantities of unusual debris—some 300 carloads of smoothly rounded stones.

In fact, the blast had revealed the world's largest natural pothole, measuring forty-two feet wide and nearly fifty feet deep. The smoothly polished stones found inside were the engines of its creation, for this, like most potholes, was the product of a whirling, abrasive slurry of sand, stones, and water that poured from a melting Ice Age glacier and steadily ground its way into the bedrock. Later, when the torrent was diverted or dried up, the monstrous hole remained, filled with the rocks that had helped to form it.

Found throughout the world in regions affected by ice age glaciation, potholes assume many shapes. Some of them widen as they grow deeper, and others bore downward at an angle, depending on the kind of rock, its composition at various depths, and the volume of water that went into the hole's creation. □

The smooth, stone-polished walls of the Archbald, Pennsylvania, pothole are evident in this 1887 photograph.

That Sinking Feeling

One balmy May evening in 1981, Mae Rose Owens was feeding her dog in front of her home on Comstock Avenue in Winter Park, Florida, when a nearby sycamore tree suddenly disappeared from sight. The tree had plunged into a newly formed hole that grew rapidly until, within less than twenty-four hours, it had swallowed Mrs. Owens's home, part of an auto-repair shop, five Porsche automobiles parked on its lots, a pickup truck, the deep end of an Olympic-size municipal swimming pool, and a stand of trees. By then, the hole was 350 feet wide and 125 feet deep, and it had devoured 160,000 cubic yards of earth—enough to fill 6,400 dump trucks.

The Winter Park chasm (above) was an exceptionally large example of a sinkhole, which occurs in areas where underground water has slowly dissolved limestone bedrock and riddled it with cavities into which the surface soil falls—taking with it whatever else is on top.

One-third of Florida is undergirded by eroded limestone at shallow depth and thus subject to sinkholes. Fortunately, disasters such as the one that struck Winter Park are relatively rare. They generally occur during dry spells, with the lowering of natural water levels in the limestone bedrock. Ground water then moves downward into the limestone cavities, carrying with it the layers of clay and sand that support the surface soil—which finally collapses.

The Winter Park sinkhole was the largest in Floridians' memory, but only one of thousands that dot the state. And Florida is not alone: Sinkhole collapse is a problem in Alabama, Pennsylvania, and fifteen other states. In Kentucky, sinkholes have created a vast area of rolling terrain. In southeastern New Mexico, lines of sinkholes connected by naturally eroded trenches march across the plain. Worldwide, particularly in China, South Africa, and the Caribbean islands, there are millions of sinkholes, some of which have created basins many miles across and pits more than 1,000 feet deep.

Geologists have no trouble identifying areas susceptible to sinkhole collapse, and they estimate that 15 percent of the earth's surface rests on such terrain. But, as the residents of Winter Park have learned only too well, science has yet to learn how to predict or prevent a sinkhole's sudden, disastrous collapse. □

Deadly Rocks

Now still, the deadly river of rock *(above)* that crashed with huge chunks of ice down Peru's Nevado de Huascaran on January 10, 1962, covers six mountain villages and their 4,000 inhabitants. The avalanche was triggered by a colossal block of glacial ice that broke free from the mountain's north peak. Eight years later, an earthquake created an even larger avalanche on the mountain, hurling 3-ton boulders 2,000 feet across the valley and rolling the one at right—weighing 15,000 tons and standing 45 feet high—several miles. The earthquake killed 25,000 people. □

Rock Music

In 1890, an inventive musician by the name of J. J. Ott put on a concert for the Buckwampum Historical Society in Bucks County, Pennsylvania. According to one member of the audience, "the clear, bell-like tones" of Ott's instrument dominated the brass band that accompanied him—a singular achievement indeed, since Ott was playing rocks.

For centuries it has been known that certain rocks can ring like a bell; there is even evidence that the ancients tapped on melodious stalactites to punctuate religious ceremonies. But some of the musical properties of ringing rocks, as they are called, seem to defy the physical laws that govern the resonating properties of more conventional instruments, such as bells.

For instance, size and shape appear to have little effect on the rocks' tone; chips off some blocks ring just like the original rock, and individual rocks may have a range of frequencies, depending on where they are struck. Most perplexing, however, is that while one rock will ring, an apparently identical neighbor often will not.

In 1965, a group of scientists set out to solve those mysteries, using boulders from a field in Upper Black Eddy in Bucks County, Pennsylvania—the probable source of J. J. Ott's instrument. The field is a rich source of ringing rocks, and over the years local residents have sought to explain the music by concocting a number of theories, some of the more extravagant ones based on witchcraft or extraterrestrial forces.

After cracking, sawing, and crushing samples of the 180-million-year-old boulders and examining them under microscopes, the researchers concluded that the ringing rocks acquired their properties from internal tension caused by alternate wetting and drying in the sunlit field. Nearby boulders that lay in the shade—either at the edge of the field or in the adjacent woods—retained more moisture, weathered more rapidly, and failed to ring. Removed from their drier environs, the ringing rocks would soon lose their musical qualities, this group of scientists concluded.

Others, however, have disputed those findings, asserting that some rocks continue to ring even when they have been submerged in a pond or kept in a damp cellar and that, further, only about one-third of the sunlit boulders actually ring. Although the scientists may have helped explain the mechanics of ringing, the challengers said, they had failed to explain conclusively why some rocks ring while their neighbors are silent.

Whatever the reasons for their sounding, ringing rocks occur throughout the world. So-called stone gongs are found in temples and homes in the vicinity of Kufow in northeastern China. Bell tones have been produced by slabs of stone found in England, Wales, Nigeria, and East Africa. □

Sounding Sands

To the people who dwell in Egypt's Sinai Desert, the eerie, haunting sound that sometimes rolls off the sand dunes suggests the calling of a *djinn*, or spirit of the dead. Arab wise men wrote about this awesome sound 1,500 years ago; this century's sages, seeking an explanation for the peculiar noise, have taken to the desert with microphones and seismic recorders. But the musical sands, as they are called, still manage to elude complete understanding.

Although investigators do not know why, they have found that, under certain conditions, dry, smooth-faced grains of sand flowing loosely down a dune emit a loud, low-frequency sound, like that produced by a kettle-drum or distant thunder. Indeed, one possible explanation is that the noise is a kind of thunder, caused by the discharge of static electricity produced by friction among moving sand particles.

Whatever the mechanism, musical sands are heard throughout the world, from the Sahara and the Sinai Desert to the deserts of South America, China, and California. Some scientists maintain that they may even sound across the arid dunes of Mars. □

The Racetrack's Slithering Stones

Visitors to California's Death Valley have long been intrigued by the so-called Racetrack, one of the barren dry lake beds, or playas, that dot the valley. The Racetrack gets its name from the flat-bottomed stones *(right),* some weighing as much as a hundred pounds, that move across the surface and leave behind long-lasting grooves that can stretch as far as thousands of feet.

For years, however, no one had actually seen the stones move, or explained how they might do so. Then, in 1967, Robert Sharp, a California Institute of Technology professor of geology, determined that the stones are propelled by forces no more mysterious than wind and water. Even a light rainfall, Sharp found, can coat the lake bed with a moist film so slippery that a strong gust will send stones scuttling. □

Mima Mounds

In 1842, the American explorer and naval officer Charles Wilkes came upon a vast field of earthen mounds on the Mima Prairie south of Puget Sound in western Washington *(left).* Scores of feet in diameter, often standing head high, the mounds were surrounded by cobblestones as large as footballs. When Wilkes dug into a few of the mounds, he found that they consisted of fertile, black prairie soil mixed with walnut-size pebbles.

Wilkes concluded that the mounds were the work of local Indians and noted that such a huge project "would have required the united efforts of a whole tribe." Later theorists, however, had different ideas. When Louis Agassiz, the great nineteenth-century zoologist and geologist, heard of the mounds, he proclaimed them to be fish nests, presumably left over from a distant past when Puget Sound covered the prairie. Others have suggested that they are the remnants of up-rooted trees or even gopher mounds. And some geologists hold that the Mima mounds are simply a product of the last ice age, about 12,000 years ago. According to one such explanation, cracks formed between frozen blocks of soil and water from melting glaciers widened the spaces, washing away all but the largest cobblestones; finally, mounds were created among the cobbles when the blocks melted and released their burdens of gravelly soil.

Although this may seem to be a reasonable explanation for the Puget Sound formations, it does not account for Mima-like mounds that appear elsewhere in the world, primarily in the western United States but also in Argentina and South Africa.

Many of these so-called pimple mounds occur far from regions that were affected by ice age glaciation. And, according to some geologists, the mounds may indeed be the work of gophers or other such burrowing rodents. □

Earth Cookies

One fall morning in 1984, Rick and Peter Timm were rounding up cattle on the family ranch in Washington State when they found a perplexing, two-foot-thick slab of earth lying atop the table-flat wheat field. Like a divot hacked out by a gargantuan golfer, the slab lay right side up, its neatly severed edge surrounded by a dribble of soil particles. It measured ten feet long and seven feet wide, and weighed about three tons.

The chunk appeared to be an exact fit for the smooth-walled hole that the Timm brothers found next, seventy-three feet away. Except for the fact that the surrounding root system was torn rather than cleanly sliced, the hole could have been made by a giant cookie cutter.

The Timms' discovery brought to seven the worldwide number of reported "cookie cutter holes"—four have been found in Norway, one in Britain, and one in Germany—but did nothing to help solve the puzzle of their creation. ◊

Observers study a 3,000-pound "earth cookie" and the hole in the ground from which it was mysteriously torn in Norway.

Theories abound: Earthquakes may have focused tremors on these spots, somehow punching up chunks of sod. Bolts of lightning might have turned the subsurface water into steam whose pressure forced blocks of earth up and out. Perhaps the ground froze and expanded, tearing the divots loose and allowing subsurface water to float them away like icebergs. In addition, methane gas explosions, meteors, and secret military experiments have been advanced to account for cookie cutter holes.

Rick Timm has his own explanation—that alien visitors landed on his ranch and somehow extracted the section of earth he and his brother discovered. Says he: "It really would've been something to be there when it happened." □

Bedrock Crude

Geodes—crystalline nodules with hollow centers—are highly prized by rock hounds and gem collectors for the delicate, beautiful structures that are often found inside them. But whatever crystals reside in the heart of the gray geodes *(right)* that sometimes turn up along Tyson's Creek in Illinois are obscured by a second presence: rank globs of crude oil and tar.

The oil-bearing Illinois geodes have no economic significance. But they—and similar finds in California, Iowa, and El Salvador—baffle geologists, who have not been able to account for the presence of petroleum.

Geodes are formed by minerals that crystallize inside enclosed cavities in rock. They grow inward, and their hollow cores are thought to be sealed from the outside. Oil and tar, on the other hand, are formed by the decomposition of organic matter—ancient leaves, trees, and marine life—under high pressure and temperature.

These two processes, according to geological teaching, do not occur together. Somehow, though, the oily geodes seem to have gathered and enclosed petroleum from the surrounding rock. □

The world's highest rock pinnacle, Ball's Pyramid, juts 1,843 feet out of the Pacific near Lord Howe Island, 500 miles east of Sydney. The longest side of its triangular base measures only 660 feet.

Like a wall of surf curling above the shore, Australia's forty-five-foot-high Wave Rock seems to hover in breathtaking suspension. This rock formation acquired its shape and its rusty hue from the action of mineral-rich waters flowing over its granite crest.

Flexible Rocks

Although rock is widely regarded as a symbol of unyielding strength, certain rocks are so pliant that a thin strip taken from them will sag under its own weight. The most common is a type of sandstone called itacolumite *(left)*, which takes its name from Itacolumi, a mountain in Brazil where it occurs in large quantities. It is also found in North Carolina, the Ural Mountains of Russia, and India.

The mechanism of the sagging is imperfectly understood. The sand grains that make up the rock are widely separated rather than closely packed as in conventional sandstones, and scientists speculate that this permits them to move about. It is not known what causes the separation, nor has anyone found a use for such a material, whose properties are so much at odds with expectation. □

Great Balls of Stone

In December 1967, archaeologist Matthew Stirling was struggling across the wild, wooded mountains of west central Mexico on horseback when, topping a ridge, he beheld a breathtaking sight. There, strewn across the rocky arroyos and partially buried in the earth, were hundreds of stone spheres, some of them as large as eleven feet in diameter *(right)*. "The scene suggested some giant's bowling alley or the ballpark of the Aztec gods," he later said.

It was not the first time that Stirling had seen such huge balls of stone. While on an expedition to Costa Rica a few years before, Stirling had uncovered a cache of granite spheres that had been carved to near-perfect roundness by ancient workers.

Stirling had been led to believe that he would find similar artifacts in Mexico's Sierra de Ameca, fifty miles west of Guadalajara. But now, as he examined the Mexican balls, he was surprised to see that they were nothing like the Costa Rican spheres. Their surfaces were rough, not smooth and patiently crafted. They were not granite, but soft volcanic stone. And there were no scatterings of debris or tools that would provide a clue as to how they were carved.

A chance remark by a workman led to the puzzle's solution. When asked to excavate some of the buried balls for further study, the worker suggested that, instead of digging, they ride up the mountain. There, he said, they would find many more spheres lying on the surface. And indeed they did, in such numbers that Stirling concluded that the balls had been

fashioned not by human hands but by natural forces.

This was confirmed by an independent geologist's analysis of the stones and their surroundings. The spheres were formed 40 million years ago, when an avalanche of hot volcanic ash flooded the area. As it slowly cooled, the ash crystallized around nuclei, or seeds, of glass. The glass radiated gases outward from the center, causing still more material to be crystallized—and creating globes of rock within the bed of ash. Sometime later, the soft, uncrystallized material that surrounded the spheres was carried away by wind and water, leaving the hard globes lying on the surface. □

Crystalline Crosses

An opaque, ruddy, and unlovely mineral, staurolite might be ignored by all but the most dedicated rock hounds—except for the crystals' propensity to form in the shape of a cross *(left)*. Because of their distinctive appearance, staurolite crystals have been adopted as religious charms, and legends have arisen wherever they are found. In Brittany in northwest France, the crystals are said to have been dropped from heaven; in Patrick County, Virginia, they are called fairy stones—reputedly the tears of fairies who wept when they heard of Christ's crucifixion.

The mineral's name is from the Greek word *stauros,* or "cross." Its cruciform shape is caused by the crystals' atomic structure. □

Roots

Sometimes mistaken for fossilized tree roots or twigs, fulgurites *(above)* are in reality glassy tubes that are formed in sand, soil, or rock by the heat of a lightning strike. Fulgurites have been known to branch downward as far as forty feet through sand dunes. □

A Mineral Phantasmagoria

Looking like death-dealing maces abandoned by a medieval army, hundreds of curious sandstone formations once were strewn across the ground at Mount Signal, California, near the Mexican border. Many more lay buried as deep as eight feet beneath the sand. Each consisted of a ball, four to seven inches in diameter, attached to a tapering, spikelike handle up to twenty inches long. Virtually all of the handles pointed west. The unusual objects were not, in fact, antique weapons, but sand spikes—bizarre examples of a common rock formation called a concretion, created when ground sediments are deposited around a nucleus such as a twig or fossil and then cemented together by waterborne minerals. Concretions are often noted for their distinctive shapes— balls, tops, tools, bunches of grapes, peanuts, barbells, and even animal forms have been discovered. They range in size from less than an inch to more than one hundred feet long.

Although the process that creates concretions is well understood, geologists have not been able to explain why the Mount Signal sand spikes assumed their uniformly unusual shape—or their westward orientation. Unfortunately, no explanation is likely to be forthcoming, since further study of the formation has been rendered impossible. Over the years, curio hunters have stripped the area of every trace of the once-numerous oddities. □

Showers of Stones

Thirty-five million years ago, a rain of glassy stones descended on the southeastern coast of North America and the Caribbean. Again and again over eons, similar showers fell on central Europe, West Africa, the Caucasus Mountains, and the Atlantic and Pacific oceans. Finally, about 750,000 years ago, some 100 million tons of the stones pelted the Indian Ocean, Australia, and Southeast Asia.

About the year 1900, scientists realized that although the remains of these showers were widely scattered and found in geological layers that varied in age by millions of years, they had a similar composition and possibly a common origin. The stones come in many unusual shapes—sometimes they resemble buttons, sometimes barbells—but all appear to have been liquid blobs that passed through the earth's atmosphere at high speed. For that reason, Austrian geologist Franz E. Suess called them tektites, from the Greek word *tektos*, meaning "molten."

The name has stuck, but since that time, scientists have found little else about tektites on which they are able to agree. Despite decades of study, the origin of the oddly formed stones remains controversial.

For years, some researchers held that tektites are particles of molten lunar soil, splashed onto the earth by meteorites crashing into the moon. But that notion was dashed when the Apollo astronauts returned with samples of lunar rock that contain only small amounts of the tektites' principal ingredients, silica and iron.

Most scientists today believe that tektites are of earthly origin. According to one theory, erupting volcanoes shot hot lumps of matter high above the atmosphere, and tektites formed as the material plunged down and scattered across the earth. But volcanoes do not have the power needed to launch millions of tons of matter high above the earth; nor does their lava contain the same proportions of materials that make up tektites. More widely accepted is the notion that huge meteorites plowed into the earth at high speed, melting surface rock and splattering particles far and wide—over hundreds of thousands of square miles in the Australian-Asian fall.

A few researchers, though, continue to look to the moon as a likely source of tektites, calculating that the debris from lunar volcanoes could have escaped the moon's weak gravity and plunged to earth. They concede that the Apollo samples rule out the moon's surface as the birthplace of tektites, but speculate that the lunar interior might contain the right mix of materials. □

WILD WINDS

More than a dozen times in the eighteenth and the nineteenth centuries, the midday skies over New England blackened, chickens went to roost, and preachers took to their pulpits to warn of impending doom. Fortunately, these so-called dark days turned out to be nothing more than the results of wind and weather, not harbingers of divine retribution.

But wind and weather have lost none of their capacity to stir fear. The awesome power of the wind can dwarf that of the most ruinous weapons of war. Hurricanes swoop through coastal regions and destroy everything in their path; tornadoes writhe unchecked across land-scapes, leaving behind a trail of devastation. And vicious blasts of unseen wind can smash the largest plane to the ground. For all the technology of modern times, people of the late twentieth century are as much at the mercy of raging winds as their most ancient forebears were. Winds, of course, can also be benign, almost playful, wafting a few hours of springlike warmth to prairies locked in winter's grip, scribing curiously distinct circles on carefully tended farm fields, and confecting jelly roll shapes from blankets of wet snow. Weather, it seems, not only is essentially unpredictable but has a whole bagful of tricks and surprises.

2

America's Most Lethal Storm

Geographers in the late nineteenth century declared that the gradual slope of the sea bottom off Galveston, Texas, made that popular Gulf Coast resort safe from the worst effects of hurricanes. Thus it was that on Friday, September 7, 1900, tourists were still splashing in the warm surf despite ominously large waves and reports of a big storm approaching.

By early Saturday, the tide was four feet higher than normal, and water was several inches deep in the streets on the Gulf side of town. Isaac Cline, the local weather bureau chief, drove his horse and wagon along the beach, urging vacationers and residents to seek higher ground or leave the island. Some heeded his warning and crossed the long bridge to the mainland, but others remained on the shore to gawk at the spectacu-

lar surf, even as it began devouring beachside buildings.

By noon, water was five feet deep in some streets, rain was falling in sheets, and the wind was building. Galvestonians began to take Cline's warnings more seriously, but it was too late to leave the island; the road bridge and three railway trestles to the mainland were already submerged.

By 5 p.m., all of Galveston was

Survivors of the Galveston hurricane of 1900 rush to locate and bury the bodies of victims to halt the spread of disease in the ravaged city.

The 1900 Galveston, Texas, hurricane packed enough energy to run all the electric power stations in the world for four years.

awash, and the storm lashed ferociously at the city, peeling roofs from houses, felling telephone poles, and killing people with flying debris. About 6:30 p.m., the water abruptly rose four feet, drowning some people where they stood and floating many houses off their foundations. Galveston's streets were now under ten feet of turbulent water, and the wind topped 120 miles an hour.

Weatherman Cline and his family had taken some fifty neighbors into their home, one of the island's sturdiest. But at 7:30 p.m., the structure collapsed, and most of the guests were drowned. Cline and several family members, clinging to wreckage, were swept out to sea and then back again, finally coming to ground three hours later 300 yards from where they had started.

The storm subsided during the night. For those who had lived through it, the morning brought a spectacle of utter calamity. Much of the resort was a jumble of splintered debris thickly laced with human corpses. Half the houses in town were destroyed. Six thousand people had been killed in Galveston, perhaps another 6,000 outside the city. In lives lost, it was—and remains today—far and away the worst natural disaster in United States history.

Galveston was rebuilt, and a sea wall was constructed to save the city from future storms. It worked: Fifteen years later a similar hurricane struck Galveston and killed fewer than a dozen people. □

Empty Desks

As if awaiting the pupils who would not return, desks and chairs remained bolted to the floor of a Milford, Connecticut, schoolhouse after its walls and roof were blown away by the disastrous New England hurricane of 1938 *(right)*. The first hurricane to hit the region in seventy years, the storm rearranged Long Island's coastline, sent ships lurching into the streets of Providence, Rhode Island, and thrust a steeple spearlike through a church roof in Dublin, New Hampshire. It also killed 600 people; mercifully, the pupils of the Milford school were out for the day when the storm struck. □

Heavy Traffic in Tornado Alley

Mike Kuhbander of Xenia, Ohio, was having an early supper with his two children when his wife, Sheila, telephoned from the downtown beauty parlor where she worked. In urgent tones, she warned of an approaching tornado.

Kuhbander immediately began opening the windows—a normal tornado-country precaution that helps reduce twister damage by equalizing air pressure inside and out. Then he heard a piercing shriek, like the sound of thousands of nails being wrenched from the boards they anchor. As Kuhbander threw himself on top of his children, a wind filled the house with flying objects and swirling dust.

As suddenly as it had begun, the noise ceased and the wind calmed. Kuhbander looked out a window and saw a scene of devastation. In little more than three minutes, the twister had flattened 3,000 dwellings and businesses and killed 34 of Xenia's 27,000 residents *(page 34)*. All around, houses were reduced to splinters. The Kuhbanders' own home was left standing, probably because of the open windows.

In Sugar Valley, Georgia, where another tornado had struck at about the same time, nine-year-old Randall Goble was less fortunate. Rushed to a hospital after he was discovered screaming hysterically in his backyard where the storm had flung him, Randall cried to a nurse, "Tell me it was a bad dream." But Randall's parents and two sisters lay dead in the rubble of their house; for him the day was a living nightmare.

The tornadoes that devas- ◊

Little is left of downtown Xenia, Ohio, after a tornado swept through on April 3, 1974. More than 300 people were killed that day, as 148 twisters struck the midwestern United States.

tated Xenia and orphaned Randall Goble were just 2 of 148 twisters that cut an unprecedented swath of destruction across the central United States from the Gulf of Mexico to Canada within a mere twenty-four hours. Entire towns were wiped out, and thirteen states, with a total of $600 million in property damage, required federal disaster aid. Three hundred fifteen people died and 6,142 were injured. So exceptional was this outbreak that it is now known to meteorologists as the "Superoutbreak of 1974."

The cause of the havoc was a 1,000-mile-long cold front that moved eastward from the southern Rockies and wedged itself beneath hot, moist air flowing north from the Gulf of Mexico across the center of the United States. Where the air masses met, there formed a ribbon of violently churning air that stretched for hundreds of miles. These are classic tornado-spawning conditions, and they occur frequently in the area, giving it the nickname of Tornado Alley.

On this spring day, both the cold front and the converging flow of warm Gulf air were exceptionally strong. Forecasters at the National Severe Storms Forecast Center in Kansas City monitored the developments with growing apprehension. But they could do nothing except issue warnings and read with dismay the day's reports of spreading destruction. Helpless to influence the events they foresaw, the forecasters were no less touched by the force of nature than the survivor of one tornado in Kentucky. "If I live forever," she said, "I will never see anything so horrible as this again." □

Deadly Superstorm

Although tornadoes are nature's most destructive storms, their vicious lives are mercifully brief. Most last less than twenty minutes and travel less than 15 miles. But occasionally—three or four times a year in the United States—these malevolent dervishes turn into superstorms that travel 100 miles or more before they are exhausted.

Despite their small number, superstorms account for 20 percent of all tornado deaths. The deadliest, most destructive of all such twisters was the Great Tri-State Tornado that cut a 219-mile swath across Missouri, Illinois, and Indiana on March 18, 1925.

The tornado touched down in the early afternoon at Annapolis, Missouri, where it demolished every building on Main Street in twenty seconds. Moving 85 miles east to Murphysboro, Illinois, it snapped off trees, whipped water pipes out of the ground, and tossed houses and railway locomotives around as if they were toys. A man named Charles Biggs leaped out of his car into a ditch as the twister approached; moments later, the automobile bounced down the street like a ball, then popped up into the funnel, never to be seen again. Biggs made his way home, where he found his house reduced to matchsticks and 7 of his 8 daughters dead—bringing the town's total death toll to 210.

Incredibly, the tornado gained power as it spun toward DeSoto, Illinois. There it destroyed the public school, burying 125 students and teachers in the wreckage. Eighty-eight people died in the school and 30 elsewhere in DeSoto, a farming town of only 600 souls. The shrieking funnel razed every building that was more than one story high; the few trees and fence posts left standing were plastered with shredded clothing and human flesh.

Similar grisly scenes were duplicated wherever the tornado passed. The official death toll was 689; scores more disappeared without a trace in America's most devastating tornado on record. □

Residents search the ruins of Griffin, Indiana, one of many towns flattened by a supertornado whose curving path stretched 219 miles across three midwestern states (inset).

The Hidden Tornado

For the aviators and scientists of the National Oceanic and Atmospheric Administration, flying an airplane into the eye of a raging hurricane is a routine part of the hazardous job of monitoring tropical storms. But the crew of NOAA 42, flying in Hurricane Hugo on September 15, 1989, as it swept up from the Antilles to its Charleston, South Carolina, landfall, got more than they bargained for when they pointed the nose of their Lockheed Orion straight at the huge storm's eye.

NOAA 42 was piercing the wall of the eye, only a few hundred feet from the calm center of the storm, when the plane was suddenly gripped by violent forces that threatened to tear it apart. One of the four engines failed, and the sturdy Orion fell to within 800 feet of the boiling sea before it finally made it into the eye. Analyzing the hair-raising event later, astonished scientists concluded that NOAA 42 had flown into a bizarre weather anomaly: a tornado that, in defiance of conventional meteorological behavior, had developed undetected in the eye's wall, cloaking its own diabolical violence in that of the larger storm. □

Seen from an altitude of 203 miles, a swirl of windblown cloud surrounds the calm eye of a Pacific hurricane.

Looking a Tornado in the Eye

Carrying in its spinning coils the most violent winds on earth, a tornado is capable of instantly destroying whatever it touches. So abrupt and total is its fury that survivors can seldom remember the details. But on May 3, 1943, retired army captain Roy S. Hall emerged with his family from the eye of a tornado—and provided a vivid description of the capricious maelstrom that destroyed his home in McKinney, Texas, some thirty miles north of Dallas.

Hall had herded his wife and four children into a bedroom for safety just as the roaring storm bore down on them. Then the room's outside wall crumpled inward with a rending crash; the frightful experience was under way.

Abruptly, the storm ceased its dreadful shriek. It was, wrote Hall, "exactly as if hands had been placed over my ears, cutting off all sound, except for the extraordinary hard pulse beats in my ears and head, a sensation I had never experienced before." In the fearful silence, a strange, blue glow lit the trembling house.

At that moment, Hall was tossed ten feet away and buried under a shattered wall, so suddenly that he had no memory of movement. He clawed his way out of the rubble, grabbed his four-year-old daughter, and waited for his house—now off its foundation—to blow away. Then he saw a terrifying apparition.

"Something had billowed down from above, and stood fairly motionless, save for a slow up-and-down pulsation," Hall wrote later. "It presented a curved face, with the concave part toward me, with a bottom rim that was almost level. . . . It was the lower end of the tornado. We were, at the moment, inside the tornado itself!"

Hall looked up and saw what appeared to be a slick-surfaced, opaque wall about ten feet thick, surrounding a hollow column. "It resembled the interior of a glazed standpipe," Hall wrote. "It extend-ed upward for over a thousand feet, and was swaying gently and bending slowly toward the southeast. Down at the bottom, judging from the circle in front of me, the funnel was about 150 yards across. Higher up it was larger, and seemed to be partly filled with a bright cloud, which shimmered like a fluorescent light."

The whirling funnel swayed and afforded Hall a new insight: The entire column appeared to be composed of a stack of huge rings, each moving independently and causing a wave to ripple from top to bottom. As the crest of each wave reached the bottom, the funnel's tip snapped like a whip.

Horrified, Hall watched the tip flick at his neighbor's house and destroy it. "The building dissolved, the various parts shooting off to the left like sparks from an emery wheel," according to Hall.

Soon the twister continued its journey to the southeast. The Hall family emerged from the devastation virtually unscathed. At the cost of their home, they had gained from the eye of a great storm a rare glimpse of nature's power at its most awesome. □

A mattress rests atop a telephone pole where it was thrown by a twister tearing through Dallas, Texas.

Tornado Whimsy

Tornadoes are as famous for their freakish tricks as for their ferocity. Spinning winds that reach 200 miles per hour can drive a straw into a tree trunk and cause lumber to pierce steel. At the same time, powerful interior vortexes—smaller whirlwinds within the whirlwind— are apparently responsible for smashing some objects while leaving others untouched. And currents of ascending air inside a twister can act as cushions: People, eggs, and jars of pickles have been yanked into the air only to be returned gently to earth amid the storm's fury.

Among the tales of whimsy and miracle to emerge from two centuries of tornado observations:

- The tornado that destroyed Xenia, Ohio, in 1974 *(page 33)* demolished a farmhouse and all its contents, but spared three fragile items: a mirror, a case of eggs, and a box of Christmas ornaments.

- On April 11, 1965, tornadoes swept a wide portion of the midwestern United States. In one, a Cleveland, Ohio, teenager was lifted out of his bed, carried through a window, and set down unharmed across the street, his blankets still tucked around him; another sucked an eight-month-old baby in Dunlap, Indiana, out of his collapsing house and deposited him 150 feet away with only a black eye; and in Grand Rapids, Michigan, a man was transported from his porch onto a pile of splinters—all that remained of his neighbor's house.

- On June 10, 1958, in El Dorado, Kansas, a woman was thrown out of a window and set safely down 60 feet away. Beside her fell a phonograph record of the song "Stormy Weather."

- On May 25, 1955, in Udall, Kansas, Fred Dye was snatched out of his shoes and plopped in a tree to sit out the storm; not far away a husband and wife emerged from the safety of their bedroom to discover that every other room in the house had blown away.

- West Virginia's West Fork River was briefly sucked dry by a tornado on June 23, 1944.

- Shortly after a devastating tornado passed through Tamaroa, Illinois, on March 18, 1925, a page from the *Literary Digest* fluttered to the ground. It contained a photograph and description of a 1917 whirlwind.

- A light-fingered twister entered the Newsome family home in Lorain, Ohio, on June 28, 1924, and stripped it bare of curtains, pictures, and furniture. The house was left intact, and the Newsomes suffered only minor cuts.

- On March 27, 1890, a twister killed 106 people and caused widespread damage in Louisville, Kentucky. The city hall was spared—but only briefly. Moments after the storm passed, it reversed course, as if it had forgotten something, and smashed the building to bits. □

Devilish Dust

Out of a cloudless blue sky on the afternoon of May 29, 1902, a whirlwind appeared and demolished a livery stable in downtown Phoenix, Arizona. The very next day a similar wind tore the roof off a local store. Both winds were extraordinarily powerful examples of dust devils, the ubiquitous swirling columns of air that tease the flat, dusty ground of the desert and prairie.

Dust devils are offspring of the sun's rays. As the ground absorbs the rays and is warmed, it heats the air immediately above, causing it to expand, rise, and swirl like a mirror image of water running down a drain. Made visible by the dust, sand, and debris swept up from the ground, dust devils zigzag across the plain, propelled at speeds of four to five miles per hour by the movement of the air around them. They commonly rise to a height of a hundred feet, although they sometimes reach several hundred feet.

A short-lived phenomenon, dust devils usually cause no damage—until a rare combination of forces creates the kind of destructive whirlwind that struck Phoenix. □

Rain of Fire

On the night of June 14, 1960, as retired school superintendent George Truett Day recalled later, the peaceful Texas community of Kopperl turned into "what Hell might be like." Few of Day's neighbors disagreed. During that memorable night, Kopperl experienced a bizarre storm in which the sky seemed to rain fire.

The evening began pleasantly enough, with cooling breezes flowing off nearby Lake Whitney. Then strange, tumbling clouds swept in, crackling with "explosive rays of lightning" like nothing Kopperl's frightened residents had ever seen. Soon, blistering air driven by hurricane-force winds pushed the temperature up to nearly 140 degrees Fahrenheit. Ears of corn were roasted on their stalks, cotton plants wilted, and fields of grass became dry hay ready for baling. Sleeping families awoke gasping for breath, and parents tried to cool their panicky children by wrapping them in wet sheets.

The next morning, Kopperl's residents phoned friends and relatives living in towns close by—and discovered that they alone had been affected by the freak heat. Those in nearby towns noted nothing unusual about their weather.

The storm remains a meteorological mystery. Without the help of accurate measurements or the reports of trained observers, scientists have been unable to provide any explanation more satisfying than that of one woman who experienced the night: "It was an act of God, I guess." □

Bay of Death

Bangladesh's Bay of Bengal may be the home of the world's deadliest weather. Since 1822, sixty cyclones have swept through the area, killing 1.6 million people.

The bay itself is a natural storm funnel, designed for disaster. Cyclones born in the Indian Ocean are fueled by the bay's warm waters. As the storms churn toward land, their waves are squeezed ever more tightly into the narrow northern end, creating huge storm surges. In some storms, a massive wall of water as high as fifty feet has swept over thousands of square miles, washing away people, livestock, and buildings. The most calamitous of these storms in modern times was an enormous cyclone that struck on November 13, 1970, killing a million people.

The deadly effects of the storms themselves are magnified by poverty and overpopulation. More than 100 million people crowd Bangladesh, a land roughly the size of Wisconsin. Theirs is the world's poorest nation: The average annual income is only $130 per person. Desperate for land on which to grow their meager subsistence crops, millions of Bangladeshi live on newly formed alluvial islands, called chars, formed by the sediments of rivers that empty into the Bay of Bengal. No sooner is a char raised above the tide than it is occupied—setting the stage for the next disaster. Warning systems and evacuation procedures are unlikely to help the delta-dwellers when the moment arrives: Few of them have radios to hear the alerts. Despite the terrible toll exacted by storm surges, the chars continue to attract settlers. The population grows by 3 million hungry people every year, and most of them have no choice but to take their chances in Bangladesh's murderous cyclone zone. ☐

The Man Who Rode the Thunder

Marine pilot William Rankin was flying over the North Carolina coast in August 1959, when suddenly his jet fighter's engine failed. The plane uncontrollable, Rankin's survival instincts kicked in. At 46,000 feet, he bailed out and dropped into the heart of a thunderstorm raging below him.

Rankin's parachute opened just as he entered the top of the storm. Instantly, "I was in an angry ocean of boiling clouds, blacks and grays and whites, spilling over each other, into each other, digesting each other," he later wrote. "I became a veritable molecule trapped in the thermal pattern of a heat engine . . . , buffeted in all directions—up, down, sideways, clockwise, counter-clockwise, over and over. I . . . zoomed straight up, straight down. I was . . . stretched, slammed and pounded. I was a bag of flesh and bones crashing into a concrete floor. . . . I didn't want to see what was going on. I kept my eyes shut, tight. This was nature's bedlam, a black cageful of screaming . . . lunatics, beating me with big flat sticks, roaring at me, . . . trying to crush me. . . . Sometimes the rain was so dense and came in such swift, drenching sheets, that I thought I would drown in mid-air."

Rankin was pummeled like this for a full forty minutes before finally dropping through the base of the cloud, 300 feet from the ground. Mercifully, his parachute snagged in a tree and swung him gently to the ground—bruised, lacerated, frostbitten, and suffering from shock. □

Microburst, Macrohazard

Summer thunderstorms darkened the skies over New York City late on the afternoon of June 24, 1975, as scores of crowded airliners converged on the city's busy John F. Kennedy International Airport. At 3:44 p.m., Eastern Airlines Flight 66 from New Orleans joined a queue of a dozen aircraft scheduled to land on Kennedy's Runway 22 Left. Twenty minutes later, eleven of those planes had landed safely. Then, at 4:05, Flight 66 plowed into the ground less than half a mile short of the runway—113 of its 124 passengers and crew killed by a sudden, powerfully concentrated, nearly invisible downward blast of air known as a microburst.

A microburst is a descending mass of heavy, cold air released by a "mature" thunderstorm—one that has stopped growing and is producing heavy rain. Microbursts are relatively small—no more than two and a half miles in diameter—but some are so powerful that experts feel that no airplane can fly through them close to the ground without crashing. The downdraft fans out when it nears the ground, sometimes forming a curling rim of wind—much like the head of an inverted mushroom—that can disrupt a plane's aerodynamics so suddenly and severely that a pilot loses control. These outflowing winds have been clocked at up to 168 miles per hour. Worse, microbursts strike without warning; they are invisible to weather radar.

As investigators later reconstructed the crash of Flight 66, a

A dust cloud *(left center)* at the edge of a dark shaft of rain marks the presence of a microburst generated by a severe thunderstorm over northern Arizona.

powerful microburst dropped out of the storm just as the aircraft entered the final stages of its landing approach. The plane flew straight into the burst's center and was immediately pushed downward. Then a gust gripped it from behind, causing the airspeed to fall nearly 20 miles per hour to a dangerously slow 140 miles per hour. As the plane dropped faster, the pilots raised the nose and applied all available power, but Flight 66 plunged to the ground only seconds after its encounter with the microburst began. □

Wave clouds stream eastward from the crests of the Rocky Mountains, shaped by the strong west winds that sometimes produce chinooks.

Spring's Playful Kiss

On the morning of January 22, 1943, spring visited the Black Hills of South Dakota in the form of a dry, warm wind known as a chinook. It toyed with the temperature "like a playful lover," as one observer wrote, before bitter winter returned once more to the region.

In the little town of Spearfish, the temperature shot from four degrees below zero to forty-five above in two minutes—such a rapid change that plate-glass windows cracked throughout town. But the chinook's effect was not felt everywhere. While temperatures soared to fifty-five degrees in Rapid City's Canyon Lake neighborhood, some downtown thermometers still sat near zero. And although it was springlike on the south side of the Alex Johnson Hotel, around the corner on the east side winter chill prevailed. In the town of Lead, the warm wind pushed the temperature to fifty-two degrees, but less than three miles away, Deadwood continued to freeze at sixteen below. Motorists crossing from winter into spring discovered that frost formed almost instantly on their chilled windshields.

Thermometers fluctuated crazily. By 9 a.m., just ninety minutes after the rapid warming began, Spearfish was shivering again at four below zero. Between 10:30 a.m. and 2 p.m., the Rapid City ◊

utility company's thermometer made four round trips between nine and fifty degrees.

Chinook winds are formed when masses of humid air cross the Rocky Mountains. Dry air making the same passage cools as it rises and expands, then regains its original temperature as it compresses during its descent on the other side. But rising humid air, in releasing moisture in the form of rain or snow, creates heat that retards the cooling process; then, as the newly dried air rushes down the mountainsides, it warms rapidly to the temperatures that led Plains Indians to call the chinook "the snow eater."

The erratic pattern of heat and cold on this January day in the Black Hills was the product of the bumpy topography of the area, which created ripples in the chinook's flow and made it dip down through the frigid surface air in some places but not in others.

Spring's courtship was brief, however. The next day, temperatures everywhere in the Black Hills hovered around zero. □

A Darkness at Noon

Late on the morning of May 19, 1780, farmers and city dwellers from New Jersey to Maine looked skyward with apprehension. As high noon approached that Friday, the sky grew dark, and the world took on a strange, brassy hue.

So far that spring, there had been little to cheer the rebellious American colonists in their war for independence from British rule. Their beleaguered army seemed to be on the verge of mutiny; now, some citizens saw the lowering gloom as an omen of worse things to come. It was a Friday, after all, the day of Christ's crucifixion, when the skies also darkened at noon. Candles were lit and prayers offered throughout the Northeast. Chickens went to roost, frogs croaked, and evening birds sang. In Hartford, the Connecticut House of Representatives adjourned. But in a nearby room, the governor's council stubbornly persisted in the gloom, urged on by one Colonel Abraham Davenport. "Either the day of judgment is at hand or it is not," he thundered. "If it is not, there is no cause for adjournment. If it is, I wish to be found in the line of my duty."

By midafternoon, the sky brightened somewhat, prayer ceased, and commerce and politics resumed. In the days that followed "Black Friday," old timers in New England recalled other occasions when the sky had darkened—including one memorable November Sunday in 1716, when the sky seemed to descend like God's wrath on the morning's religious services.

There were, however, some clues pointing to a natural cause for the onset of these ominously darkened skies: Rainfall at such times was often sooty and laden with bits of burned leaves. In time, scientists who studied the phenomenon theorized that the strange darknesses in the eastern part of the country might be caused by vast forest fires raging unchecked in the unpopulated western territories.

The assumption proved correct. Moreover, the normal west-to-east flow of wind and weather made New England particularly susceptible to dark days. Typically, soot and smoke from western fires rose high into the sky, where they were drawn into developing storm systems, hovering unseen above the lower clouds. Since many of the systems travel down the St. Lawrence Valley on their way to the ocean, the gloom descended most frequently on southern Canada and New England.

Dark days were recorded eighteen times between 1706 and 1910. In later years, deforestation and fire prevention efforts all but eliminated them. □

High winds at sea can whip up gigantic waves. Sailors of the Imperial Japanese Fleet caught in a Pacific typhoon on September 26, 1935, observed some of the biggest waves ever reported—up to ninety feet, as high as a nine-story building.

Ill Winds

When the foehn, or warm wind, blows off the mountains of southern Germany, Switzerland, and Austria, it brings with it a host of physical and emotional symptoms. People report aching joints, throbbing headaches, nausea, fatigue, apathy, irritability, and depression. Traffic accidents become more frequent. Doctors sometimes postpone surgery; the foehn is said to increase the likelihood of hemorrhage, thrombosis, and embolism.

As many as half of all Germans consider themselves to be *wetterfühlig*, or weather sensitive. Their discomfort rises immediately before the onset of a foehn, when the temperature rises and the humidity drops precipitously. The gullible turn for relief to a wide variety of products available from druggists and mail-order merchants—including magnetic bracelets, necklaces, and innersoles. With or without the aid of nostrums, the symptoms tend to fade as the wind attains full force.

The foehn is just one of the world's "ill winds," blamed for all sorts of human illness and upset. The Israelis call theirs the *sharav;* the Arabs have the *chamsin.* Similarly, France has its *autun,* and Yugoslavia the *koschava.* Although each wind owes its origin to different factors of weather and terrain, all are hot, dry, and uncomfort-able. In California, the Santa Ana wind roars into Los Angeles off the desert, ushering in—as writer Joan Didion once put it—a "season of suicide and divorce and prickly dread." Statistics do not bear out her assertion about suicide and divorce, but Angelenos have reason to dread the Santa Ana. The wind, which sometimes exceeds the strength of a hurricane, shoves trucks off roads and fans forest fires. Doctors report an increase in pulmonary problems and bloody noses, for which the Santa Ana's extremely low humidity—as low as two percent—is usually blamed.

The connection between wind, weather, and health has been made at least since the time of Hippocrates, the Greek father of medicine. He claimed a two-way linkage: Not only did certain winds bring on specific illnesses, but diseases could be used to forecast the weather. For example, Hippocrates taught that mouth sores were a herald of warm southern winds and that the winds themselves brought headaches and torpor.

Modern meteorology has discredited the Greek's weather forecasting techniques. And medical researchers—whose studies have produced conflicting and controversial results—remain skeptical about the true effect of wind on health. But the notion of "ill winds" remains as persistent as the wind itself. □

Shifting Sands

Although sand covers less than 20 percent of the earth's deserts, the graceful, windblown sand dune serves in popular imagination as a symbol for all deserts. Dunes assume many forms, but three basic shapes can be found worldwide— each determined by topography and patterns of wind flow. For example, linear dunes are characteristic of much of Australia's interior. Roughly aligned with the direction of the strong, steady prevailing winds, the desert dunes look from high in the air like furrows in freshly plowed fields. Crescent dunes—once known by their more exotic Russian name, barchan—are symmetrical shapes that frequently march across a desert as rapidly as fifty feet per year, their downwind-pointing horns leading the way. Most troublesome to travelers are fields of closely packed star-shaped dunes. Formed by shifting winds and resembling curling starfish with high-heaped central points, these ever-changing sand mountains may grow to higher than 1,500 feet.

The size and variety of desert dunes present a constant danger to travelers, who risk disorientation among the valleys of sand. Nowhere is the risk greater than in China's 130,000-square-mile Takla Makan desert, one of the world's sandiest. The name Takla Makan translates as "once you go in, you can never come out." □

The Power of Underground Air

Now covered over, the so-called Drumming Well at Oundle, in central England, earned widespread fame in the seventeenth and eighteenth centuries by producing a sound uncannily like "strokes upon a drum." Moreover, the well is said to have drummed in anticipation of events that were of great importance to England. The deaths of King Charles II and King James II, as well as several battles with France, were supposedly preceded by long, sonorous drummings that often continued for days at a time. Soldiers who once camped near the well even claimed that the beats were drummed in time to a particular march.

Investigations revealed that the well, nearly forty feet deep and situated on the side of a hill, produced its characteristic cadence only when filled with between six and eleven feet of water. Observers writing about the phenomenon speculated that when heavy rains caused the water level to rise rapidly, pockets of air were trapped in underground fissures just beyond the well's wall. Eventually forced out, the air bubbled to the surface of the water, creating a gurgling sound that resonated in the long hole.

Unusual wells are not merely the province of history and legend. In central Oregon there are scores of wells and caves whose noises result from air circulation deep underground. The area is riddled with millions of interconnected cracks and cavities, none larger than a fingernail, formed when volcanic lava shrank as it cooled. Because the region is geologically quite young—no more than seven million years old—the tiny spaces have not yet filled in with soil and minerals. Air swirls through the underground labyrinths but is trapped between impenetrable layers of fine-grained earth. Where wells and caves penetrate the surface, the underground air reacts to changes in atmospheric pressure; when the pressure rises, air rushes into the ground, and when it falls, as it does just before a storm, air races out of the earth. At the mouths of some wells, it creates updrafts so strong that objects thrown into their centers are lifted up and borne back out.

Capping a well or covering a cave forces the air to squeeze through tiny holes or crevices in the cover, producing all kinds of noises. The Lavacicle Cave, in central Oregon, whistles and roars as it pumps thousands of cubic feet of air through cracks around its quarter-inch-thick steel cover.

Kathy Miller of Bend, Oregon, has put one such blowing well to good use. One pipe connects the well to her house, another to a greenhouse. Because the air that surges from the well maintains a constant temperature of fifty-five degrees Fahrenheit, it is used in winter to heat the greenhouse, enabling vegetables and fruits to flourish while temperatures outside dip as low as twenty-five degrees below zero. In summer, air from the same source cools both the house and the greenhouse. □

Snow Rollers

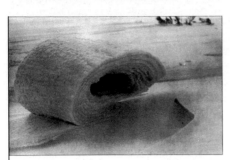

Like an invisible, playful child, a strong wind can lift a thin layer of wet snow to create the jelly roll shape of a snow roller *(left)*. Scores of snow rollers cover frozen lakes and fields under the right conditions of high wind, warm air, and sticky snow. □

Glorious Morning Clouds

Many mornings in the north of Australia, the sun rises into a cloudless sky over the great Gulf of Carpentaria. But sometimes, especially in the predawn of spring mornings, a solitary, rolling cloud stretches from horizon to horizon, sweeping low, fast, and purposefully across the brightening sky. As it passes, a gusty wind is felt, sometimes some mist, and then the cloud is gone. The Morning Glory, this cloud is called *(below)*.

To meteorologists, the Morning Glories of Carpentaria—the likes of which are found nowhere else in the world—are a persistent puzzle, much studied but little understood. As many as seven of the clouds in succession have been seen to sweep the sky, each one only a few hundred feet thick but extending seventy-five miles or more in length.

Australian scientists, who have analyzed the air pressure, moisture, wind direction, and speed of the Morning Glory, theorize that the cloud results when dry winds flowing off the Cape York Peninsula collide with opposing moist air over the gulf. The resulting swirl, they say, could produce the rolling Morning Glory. □

Circles of flattened grain, precisely carved by an unseen force, overlie the tracks of farm machinery on an English field.

Spun Cereals

Late one July afternoon in 1982, Ray Barnes was walking his two dogs along a country lane near the village of Westbury on the edge of England's Salisbury Plain. A brief thunderstorm had just passed, and as Barnes strolled through a light drizzle, he spied signs of a peculiar wind making its way across a nearby field of grain. This "invisible agency," as he later called it, swept in a line across the field before abruptly stopping, pivoting on one end, and with a "hiss and rustle," neatly flattening a circle of grain 100 to 150 feet in diameter. The entire event took just a few seconds before the mysterious "agency" vanished.

What Ray Barnes saw that July afternoon was the formation of one of England's crop circles—enig-

matic patterns of flattened grain that have been reported in growing numbers since they began to receive scientific attention in the early 1980s.

More like the work of sculptors than of destructive forces, the circles are neatly inscribed on fields bearing crops ranging from soybeans to sugar beets. Most often, however, the circles appear in wheat, barley, and oats—all cereal crops. They appear as single circles, concentric rings, groups of circles forming Celtic crosses and other patterns, and even, in one instance, a tadpole formed by a circle with a long, curling tail. The edges of the patterns are precisely formed, and the flattened grain is laid down carefully in a neat spiral. Even more curiously, in cases of concentric circles the direction of the spiral is reversed in each suc-

ceeding circle. Since 1980, more than 800 crop circles have been reported in Britain, including 300 in 1989 alone.

Neither Ray Barnes's detailed account of one circle's formation nor hordes of instrument-bearing scientists have answered all of the questions surrounding the circles. The counties of Wiltshire and Hampshire, in which most have been spotted, are not far from Britain's mysterious megalithic stone circles at Avebury and Stonehenge. Not surprisingly, therefore, enthusiasts have offered various supernatural and paranormal explanations, among them alien spaceships and mysterious electromagnetic forces. Helicopters, enraged hedgehogs, and rutting deer have also been proposed.

After nearly a decade of study, British meteorologist George Ter-

ence Meaden has come up with a far less exotic theory. He speculates that weather and topography conspire to create vortexes, or compact miniwhirlwinds, not unlike those that spin off the wingtips of airplanes. Aircraft vortexes are set in motion when the high-pressure air below the wing is sucked around the plane's wingtip by the low-pressure air above. The resulting spiral, while short-lived, can have great force—enough so that the vortex from the wing of a large plane can upset a small one that flies into its path.

According to Meaden, hills, woods, and other features of the terrain can have a similar effect on the wind blowing across them, so vortexes form that are powerful enough to flatten grain in a confined area and, on occasion, create concentric rings. □

Tornadoes of Fire

One of America's most stunning catastrophes—a pair of gigantic firestorms that drove flaming whirlwinds through a number of Wisconsin and Michigan towns in 1871—is also one of the least remembered. Although the fires killed a thousand or more people, memory of the event was eclipsed by another, unrelated disaster that struck elsewhere the same night.

It was a dry autumn in the upper Midwest. There had been no rain since July 8, and for weeks small blazes had plagued the loggers and sawmill operators in the pine forests along Green Bay near the border of Wisconsin and Michigan. On Sunday, October 8, an ominous yellow veil of smoke hid the sun over Peshtigo, Wisconsin. Residents of the lumber town did not know that a rising wind had united the scattered blazes into a single conflagration that was advancing on them like an army of fire.

That evening, they heard its ominous roar swelling in the southwest. Then, shortly after 9 p.m., a massive storm of fire struck Peshtigo. "Houses crumpled like paper," wrote one reporter, "and flaming roofs were borne away like gigantic sparks upon the fiery gale." The air itself became incendiary, and people died simply from inhaling it. The hair and clothing of others burst into flame. Hundreds crowded into the Peshtigo River, fighting for space to submerge themselves between breaths.

Storekeepers lowered merchandise into wells in hope of saving it—unwittingly condemning the children who were lowered into the same wells minutes later, then burned to death when the goods below them went up in flames.

Survivors described the onrushing blaze as a "tornado of fire." The account of Alfred Griffin, who lived near Peshtigo, was typical: "When I heard the roar of the approaching tornado I ran out of my house and saw a great black, balloon-shaped object whirling through the air over the tops of the distant trees." Modern analysis demonstrated that Griffin did indeed see a whirlwind spawned not by weather but by fire. From experiments and the study of vast fires ignited in World War II bombing raids, scientists have learned that large, intense blazes can create massive updrafts and hurricane-force surface winds. These, in turn, spawn powerful vortexes—tornado-like whirlwinds.

Peshtigo was the largest town destroyed: 750 people or more died there. Another fire simultaneously swept up the Door Peninsula—now a placid resort area on the other side of Green Bay—and between them the two fires devastated twenty-three towns and villages, badly damaged eighteen others, and leveled hundreds of isolated farmsteads. Estimates of deaths range as high as 1,500, and 1.3 million acres of timberland were burned.

But news of the Peshtigo Horror, as it eventually came to be called, was not to rivet the attention of the nation. On the very same night, several hundred miles to the south, a blaze was started that burned much of Chicago. Although the Peshtigo Horror took five times as many lives, it was ever after hidden in the shadow of the Great Chicago Fire. □

THE FALLING SKIES

Many ordinary people had long known what the members of the distinguished French Academy of Science acknowledged in 1803—that rocks fall from the sky. Reason, it seems, had forced the institution, a bastion of world scientific opinion, to deny reality. Thirteen years earlier, stones had showered down on a part of southern France, breaking branches off trees and shattering roof tiles. Although 300 of the alarmed inhabitants swore in an affidavit that they had witnessed the event, their account was dismissed out of hand: Such a phenomenon, said the scientists, was "*physically* impossible." But when a similar shower of what were later acknowledged to be meteorites occurred in 1803, some seventy miles from Paris, and was widely observed, the academy had to yield in its opinion. Here was positive proof that extraterrestrial objects do indeed hurtle down from the heavens.

Many other unexpected things fall to earth from the skies. Raindrops of various hues, large chunks of strangely shaped ice, bits of uncertain organic matter—all have been known to drop down in the midst of wondering observers. And strangest of all, perhaps, are the showers of living fish, frogs, and other squirming creatures that have been documented around the world.

As the fascinating data continues to accumulate, one thing is certain: The sky overhead contains more mysteries, more anomalies, than anyone ever dreamed.

3

Star Struck

Although virtually all of the two million or so meteors that enter the earth's atmosphere daily burn up or explode within twenty-five to ten miles of the ground and thus do no harm, some make it all the way down and occasionally hit someone. Even so, there are no verified reports of human fatalities caused by meteor falls. There have, however, been a number of close calls. In 1924, for example, a funeral procession in Johnstown, Colorado, narrowly escaped disaster when a meteorite landed where the mourners had passed just moments before. And in 1954 a Sylacauga, Alabama, woman had a similar close brush with death. Mrs. E. H. Hodges, who, coincidentally, lived opposite the Comet Drive-In Theater, had just drifted off to sleep on her living-room couch when she was awakened by a loud crash: An eight-and-a-half-pound meteorite had ripped through her roof, bounced off her radio, and struck her in the thigh, leaving a large bruise.

Among other documented near misses: A five-year-old Japanese girl was out playing when a small meteorite lodged in her neckband in 1927; and two Australian housewives were sunbathing at Binningup Beach in Perth in 1984 when a meteorite resembling a blackened baked potato landed in the sand beside them.

Some people claim to have been burned by matter from space. In 1955, a fiery metallic missile crashed into the bedroom of a Darby Township man in Philadelphia, searing his hand when he picked it up to throw it out the window. He was certain it was a meteorite. If in fact the object had originated in space, it would have represented the first recorded instance of a flaming meteorite reaching the ground. A local astronomer suggested that the so-called meterorite may well have been a homemade bomb. □

Chinese scientists peer into the eighteen-foot-deep crater of a meteorite that narrowly missed a village near Kirin when it plunged to earth in March 1976.

A Boom from Space

To those who have witnessed a meteor's fall, it is not just the blinding flash that is so startling, but the noise that often accompanies it. When a meteor came shrieking out of the sky over Benld, Illinois,

in 1938, people mistook it for a dive bomber. The missile pierced Ed McCain's garage, continued through the roof of his car parked there *(above)*, and penetrated the backseat and the floorboard before rebounding from the muffler.

Another meteor sailing over Ireland in April 1969 sent out a sonic boom and a shock wave that shook cars and rattled houses for miles around. In October of the same year, a meteor bore down on a Czechoslovakian farm, temporarily deafening a woman standing in a field with its airplanelike roar as it narrowly missed her and plunged into her house.

For Vietnam War veteran Don Richardson of Claxton, Georgia, a meteor hurtling from above in 1984 sounded so much like the whining of enemy mortar fire that he was about to duck when he caught sight of the stone smashing into his next-door neighbor's mailbox. □

When Meteorites Strike Twice

Within a span of eleven years, two houses in the township of Wethersfield, Connecticut, were struck by meteorites. Since only a score or so buildings anywhere in the world are known to have sustained meteorite hits in the past hundred years, the chances of this double blow were vanishingly small.

Mr. and Mrs. Paul Cassarino were still sound asleep on the morning of April 8, 1971, when the first meteorite, Wethersfield One, blasted into their second-floor apartment. Mr. Cassarino went to investigate; he discovered a pile of plaster dust on the living-room carpet and a hole in the ceiling where the 12.3-ounce meteorite had lodged itself.

On November 8, 1982, Mr. and Mrs. Robert Donoghue were watching M*A*S*H when Wethersfield Two tore into their house, ricocheted around the living room, and overturned furniture.

Both meteorites proved to be of identical composition—apparently they were fragments of the same celestial body. Why they should have fallen more than a decade apart, no one could say. □

A Wethersfield, Connecticut, fireman inspects the hole in the ceiling of Robert Donoghue's house, torn by a four-pound meteorite in 1982.

Diamonds in the Sky

The composition of meteorites includes ingredients ranging from rare metals to diamonds older than the earth and the sun. Not surprisingly, when a meteor survives its fiery entry into the earth's atmosphere, geologists and astronomers are eager to take it back to their labs and examine it.

Only twenty or so diamond-bearing meteorites have been recovered, and the diamonds within them have been so small that trillions would fit on the head of a pin. Scientists believe that such diamonds were created billions of years ago, before the formation of the solar system, when dying stars exploded and sent particles and gases flying through space.

Diamonds are not the only scientific treasure included in meteorites. On September 28, 1969, thunder—or at least it was thought to be thunder—shook a barn near Murchison, Australia, just before a black rock shot through the roof, narrowly missing two farm hands. It was subsequently sent to scientists at the U.S. National Aeronautics and Space Administration for investigation. After lengthy analysis, they made the startling announcement that the missile from space contained amino acids, the basic building blocks of proteins. The meteorite's message was unmistakable: The makings of life—if not life itself—could exist elsewhere in the universe. □

A thin-sliced cross section reveals clusters of glass and magnesium, olivine, and other minerals contained in a rare variety of meteorite that rained down on Mexico in 1969.

Thunderstone Storms

Before an understanding of the true nature of meteorites developed, many people referred to them as thunderstones, noting that they descended with a thunderlike noise, often during real thunderstorms. Not all thunderstones, however, were meteorites. Some, it is believed, were small rocks swept up by high winds and then dropped by the storms; others, found lying on the ground after thunder, may have been concretions of sand fused when lightning struck.

Among the Greeks, thunderstones of meteoric origin were held to have miraculous properties and were worn as talismans. On the island of Samos, for example, a person wearing a thunderstone was considered impervious to lightning. □

Water and Life from Space?

Raining down on earth from the heavens may be more than meteors and their detritus. Some scientists—a small minority, to be sure—believe that our oceans and even some of our illnesses may have their origins in space.

In 1986, physicist Louis Frank and colleagues from the University of Iowa proposed that the earth is under constant bombardment by icy minicomets weighing about 100 tons each. Frank believes that they exist in the solar system in such numbers that their total mass may be ten times greater than that of all the planets put together. According to Frank, these comets, which have been entering the earth's atmosphere at a rate of one every three seconds for millions of years, have released enough water to fill the oceans.

The British astronomer Sir Fred Hoyle and a colleague, Chandra Wickramasinghe of the University of Wales College of Cardiff, suggest that disease-bearing organisms are regularly seeded into the atmosphere by passing comets and that rudimentary life may have arrived on earth in just such a form four billion years ago. Hoyle and Wickramasinghe consider both colds and influenza illnesses from space, attributing the influenza outbreaks of 1957 and 1968 to debris traveling in the wake of Halley's comet, which orbits the sun every seventy-six years. They point out that three-quarters of a century earlier, there were epidemics of the same kind of flu.

Such a notion of spaceborne disease apparently is not as new as it might seem. The word *influenza* originated in the fifteenth century, when Italians attributed an epidemic of the illness to the influence of the stars. □

Large meteorites ordinarily create huge craters when they strike the earth. But the sixty-ton Hoba meteorite—the largest on record—was found in a shallow hole in Namibia in 1920 *(right)*. Scientists speculate that the friction of the earth's atmosphere slowed the meteorite's fall enough to cushion its landing.

Close Calls

The scenario is wild but possible: A meteorite thirty miles across slams into earth at a speed of 100,000 miles an hour. The resulting explosion—100,000 times more violent than all the nuclear weapons on earth exploding at once—heats the air to 3,100 degrees Fahrenheit above an area equivalent in size to Africa and leaves a crater hundreds of miles across.

No one can predict when a cosmic disaster of such magnitude might occur. But the earth itself offers ample proof that collisions of enormous magnitude have taken place in the past; some 120 meteoritic craters attest to that. The Manicouagan, among the largest, lies in northeastern Quebec; it stretches sixty miles across and is more than 200 million years old. A more recent impact, Arizona's Bar-

ringer or Meteor Crater, is a mere 20,000 years old; it is 600 feet deep and almost a mile wide. For a meteorite to have dug a hole that big, it would have to have weighed at least a thousand tons.

The effect such collisions have had on life in the surrounding areas is unknown. Some scientists have posited that a gigantic meteor 66 million years ago darkened the sky with dust thrown up when it collided with the earth, cutting off sunlight, lowering temperatures, and helping send the dinosaurs and other creatures toward extinction. Indeed, much of the earth's crust contains a layer of iridium—an element common in meteorites but rare on earth—dating from about the time that the dinosaurs died off.

The earth has experienced sever-

al near misses and one known hit from interplanetary bodies in this century. In 1908, an explosion of unknown magnitude rocked a 1,500-square-mile area of central Siberia. While trees and vegetation were flattened, there was no giant crater to suggest a meteor. Current theory suggests that a small comet exploded overhead.

In March 1989, an asteroid measuring a half-mile across and moving at 44,000 miles an hour came within 480,000 miles of the planet. Had it intersected the path of the earth, it would have left a crater five to ten miles wide and a mile deep. One astronomer estimates that the solar system contains as many as 1,500 similarly huge comets and asteroids whose courses could bring them into collision with earth. The prospect of one's coming nearer than the 1989 asteroid has had some scientists contemplating construction of a nuclear-armed rocket to nudge it away from earth into a new orbit before it can do damage. □

Barely grazing the atmosphere at about thirty-six miles above the earth, a meteor thirty feet in diameter streaks across the sky above Grand Teton National Park in Wyoming on August 10, 1972 *(left)*. The eroded Manicouagan Ring, sixty miles in diameter *(right)*, marks the spot in northeastern Quebec where a huge meteorite slammed into the earth more than 200 million years ago.

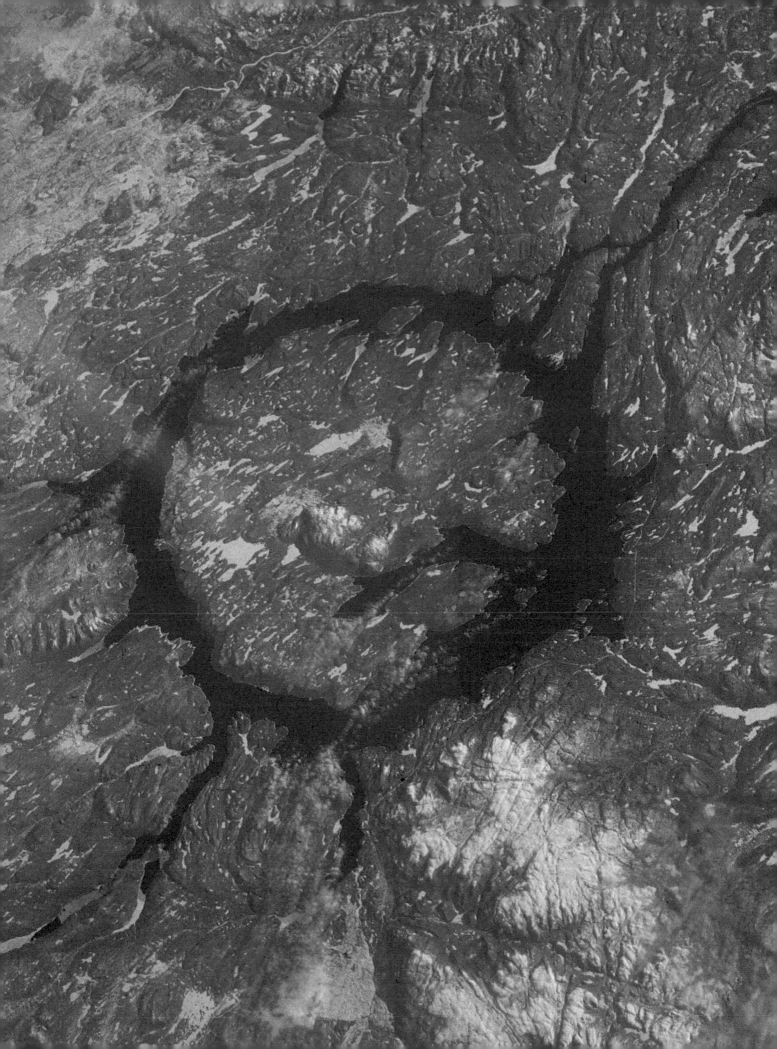

Bombarded Earth

An estimated 24,000 meteorites weighing more than 3.5 ounces each strike the earth's surface annually. This means that an average of sixty-six interplanetary rocks land somewhere every day. Two-thirds of that number, however, are lost in the oceans. In addition, an estimated 100,000 tons of cosmic dust, the remnants of burned-out meteors, drift down on the planet every year. □

A Raceway in the Sky

Comets, asteroids, and meteors are the speed demons of the solar system. The average comet moves at 129,603 miles per hour; an asteroid's average speed is 39,603 miles per hour. Using radar, astronomers have clocked one meteor whizzing along at 164,250 miles per hour. □

Mock Nuclear Blasts

When the United States signed a nuclear test-ban treaty with the Soviet Union in 1963, a secret global network of air-pressure sensors was set up to detect any clandestine aboveground nuclear blasts. Soon the sensors began registering air shocks a half-megaton in force. It did not take scientists long to figure out what was causing them: Meteors or small comets exploding in the upper atmosphere were doing so with the power of nuclear warheads. □

The Willamette Heist

In 1902, Ellis Hughes, forty-three, came upon a boulder-size meteorite embedded in the ground among pine and birch trees in the woods near his home in Willamette, Oregon. He wanted it, but there was a problem: It had landed on the property of the Oregon Iron and Steel Corporation. Convinced that the big stone would translate into big dollars for his family, Hughes nevertheless went ahead with the Herculean feat of moving it to his place.

Little did he know that he was in possession of the largest meteorite yet discovered in the United States. To budge the 13.8-ton stone, Hughes employed his fifteen-year-old son and an old horse. From the winter of 1902 to the spring of 1903, the Oregon farmer chopped his way through 4,000 feet of brush to clear a path to his farm. (He also cleared 800 feet in the opposite direction, just to confuse his neighbors.) With the path ready, he devised a system of ropes and pulleys and hoisted the massive stone onto a flatbed.

On a good day, man, boy, and horse were able to move the meteorite 150 feet. Finally, after a full year of almost incessant labor, Hughes had his prize. He then built a shed around it and began charging locals twenty-five cents each for a look.

The excitement generated by the meteorite inevitably encouraged a visit by Iron and Steel Corporation lawyers, who were none too pleased over its removal from their client's property. The company took Hughes to court, where a judge

Edward Hughes with
the meteorite that
he and his father
hauled out of the
Oregon woods.

determined, in a precedent-setting decision, that meteorites rightfully belong to the owner of the property on which they fall.

When Hughes lost an appeal in 1905, the corporation lugged the huge stone to the nearby Willamette River, floated it by barge to Portland, and put it on display at the popular Lewis and Clark Exposition. Later that year, the wife of a wealthy New York industrialist bought the meteorite for $26,000 and had it shipped to New York's American Museum of Natural History, where it resides to this day. □

Blockbusters

Hail is usually pellet-size, but hailstones of golf-ball dimensions are not uncommon—and some hail is far larger. In 1970, hail falling on Coffeyville, Kansas, delivered one stone that measured more than seventeen inches in circumference and weighed over a pound and a half, the biggest such stone ever documented by the United States National Weather Service. But it was nothing compared with the boulder-size chunk—reported to have weighed 80 pounds—that landed near Salina, Kansas, in 1882. Packed in sawdust to keep it from melting, it was taken to town and put on display.

If accounts from India set down in the nineteenth century are to be believed, there were at least four occasions when ice "many hundred pounds in weight" dropped from on high. One block, it was said, was the size of an elephant, and despite the searing heat, took three days to melt.

In more recent times, a sheet of ice weighing 14 pounds landed on a sheep in Exmoor, England, killing the animal. Another piece, estimated to weigh between 30 and 50 pounds, crashed into the third floor of a law office in Riverside, California, in 1972. One giant chunk, believed to weigh over 100 pounds, landed on the pavement in Wuxi, China, in 1983.

Explanations of the phenomenon vary. Recent falls are often attributed to the buildup—and breakup—of ice on airplanes. But planes did not exist in the nineteenth century, of course. Moreover, the Federal Aviation Administration has exonerated planes of blame in most instances; indeed, an atmospheric physicist found that only two out of thirty icefalls in the 1950s could be attributed to flights. An alternate theory proposes that the chunks form when hailstones, tumbling about in clouds, fuse with one another and then drop of their own weight. □

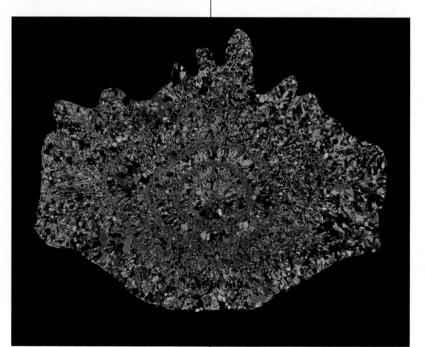

A cross-sectional photograph, taken with special polarizing filters, reveals the intricate structure of the largest American hailstone on record—a 1.67-pound lump of ice that fell on Coffeyville, Kansas, in 1970.

Candy from the Sky

Inhabitants of Peshawar, in what is today Pakistan, were used to the heavy downpours that the seasonal monsoons brought, but in the year 1893, the rains that fell on their city came accompanied by strange hail. The people who picked up shattered pieces to suck—as was the custom in the hot climate—found that the hailstones were sweet. What had given the hail its candylike flavor remains a mystery; sugary organic particles in the air may have been incorporated into the stones as they formed. □

Killer Hail

Most hailstorms send a smattering of pellets harmlessly to the ground. But they can also ravage crops, kill people and animals, and bury towns and cities under several inches of shattered ice. One of the worst hailstorms on record devastated parts of Bangladesh on April 14, 1986, with two-and-a-quarter-pound hailstones; when it ended, ninety-two people lay dead. But it pales in comparison with the lethal hailstorm that is said to have occurred in 1359, a few miles from Chartres, France. Edward III of England and his army were preparing to attack the French foe when a violent thunderstorm unleashed a bombardment of oversize hail. The bludgeoning stones killed 6,000 of Edward's horses and 1,000 of his best troops. Not even the armor some men wore offered sufficient protection from the icy blows.

Asia has had its share of killer hail. On March 28, 1867, hailstones as large as coconuts and mangoes pounded a country district near Bellary, India, and in one township alone killed two men, 2,470 sheep, and eight cattle. Trees were stripped of their foliage and clothes were torn off backs. A century later, in China, massive hailstones—some weighing as much as twelve pounds—dropped on rural districts north of Beijing and annihilated entire flocks of sheep.

Not all victims have been on the ground when hail led to disaster. On April 4, 1977, thickly falling ice forced a DC-9 to crash-land on a highway near New Hope, Georgia. The impact took sixty-eight passengers' lives. □

Colored Snow

Pink and red snow are fairly common in arctic and alpine regions: Algae living among the crystals color whole patches. But snow has been known to waft from the sky already tinted—in shades of blue, green, gray, and black. The Christmas of 1969, for example, brought black snow to a 16,000-square-mile area of Sweden. The snow apparently scrubbed the atmosphere of soot and pollution in its fall; subsequent examination of samples in laboratories revealed the presence of DDT and PCBs. In 1953, phosphorescent green snow fell near Dana, California. Residents adventurous enough to taste some of the flakes described a green persimmon flavor. Many who handled the snow developed rashes and a severe itch. When a weatherman ventured that the fall was the result of atomic testing in Nevada, the U.S. Atomic Energy Commission was quick to point out that the wind would have to have been blowing from the opposite direction for any atomic debris to have reached Dana. The source of the green flakes remains a mystery to this day. □

Snowflake Twins

No two snowflakes are ever supposed to look alike, but a Colorado researcher, Nancy C. Knight of the National Center for Atmospheric Research in Boulder, collected and photographed two identical flakes *(right)* during a research flight over Wisconsin in early 1988. They were columnar in shape, with a hole through the middle. □

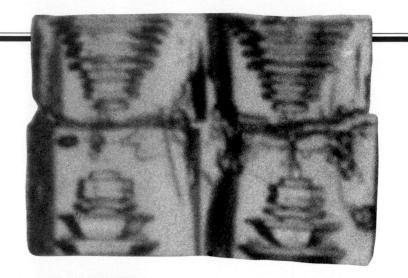

Sculpted Hail

Normally spherical, hail occasionally takes unusual shapes, ranging from cones, pyramids, and triangles to hemispheres, stars, and multifaceted crystals. Even hail resembling hats, tadpoles, and the ringed planet Saturn has been known to fall. Sometimes several kinds of hail will accompany a single storm. In 1901, hail on the St. Lawrence River near Florence Island, New York, came down as icicles, walnut-shaped knobs, and disks three inches wide and two inches thick. According to an eyewitness, the ice caused "thousands of fountains from a foot to six feet in height" to spurt up as it hit the surface of the water. □

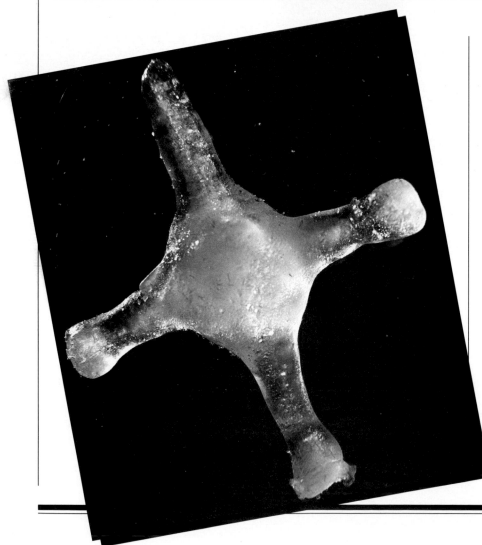

Sparking Rain

Wet though rain may be, it can emit sparks. The phenomenon has been reported from around the world. One 1892 account from Cordova, Spain, tells how a thunderstorm brought "great drops of electrical rain, each one of which, on touching the ground, walls, or trees, gave a faint crack, and emitted a spark of light." It is thought that during electrical storms lightning charges the raindrops. ☐

Manna from Heaven

The Bible tells how manna, a white, flaky substance, fell from heaven each night as the Israelites made their way across the desert. By gathering it up and baking it into bread, they were able to keep themselves from starving to death. Several theories have been put forth to explain manna. One suggests that it was the sweet excretion of insects that feed on the tamarisk trees of the region; another that it was a form of lichen wafted aloft during the day by warm winds and then deposited on the sand at night when temperatures plummeted. ☐

Rain of a Different Color

Ed Mootz of Cincinnati, Ohio, could not believe his eyes that day in July 1955, when the rain came down red. What is more, it burned him. "It felt like I had put turpentine on an open cut," Mootz said. The next day, his peach tree was dead, and the fruit was shriveled and brown *(above)*.

Why the poisonous rain was red in this instance has never been explained. But colored rain, it turns out, is more common than most people might imagine—usually the result of impurities or natural substances in the air. Yellow and green rains have occurred where pollen is particularly thick. A black rain that fell on England in 1884, turning brooks to ink, took its coloration from soot. And the red rain that occasionally falls in Europe and over the Caribbean can be traced to red Sahara sand blown into the upper atmosphere by desert storms. ☐

A Singular Downpour

When light rain fell on the village of Weston near Bath, England, late in the afternoon of June 14, 1878, no one expected a flood. Yet, amazingly enough, water was soon advancing down the main street in a four-foot-high wave—and with sufficient force to move a large, heavy stone several yards and damage houses.

The village had been the victim of point precipitation, a highly localized downpour that occurs when water-saturated storm clouds dump their moisture on one location. In this case, the rain had fallen mostly on a nearby hill, with the runoff coursing down the road into town. □

Angel Hair

Hundreds of calls began pouring into newspaper offices and police stations in St. Louis on October 8, 1969, as gossamer-like threads descended from the sky. People were worried that a test plane belonging to the local McDonnell Douglas aircraft company might have blown up, or that there was a flying saucer in the vicinity. Some even saw the shower of threads as a divine sign.

This was by no means the first time such a phenomenon had been reported. More than two centuries earlier, in 1741, people living around Selborne, England, woke one September day to find enclosures and fields draped with what appeared to be cobwebs. "The whole face of the country seemed as if it were covered with two or three setting-nets drawn one over the other," wrote a resident. "When the dogs attempted to hunt, they, blinded and hoodwinked, were obliged to lie down and scrape the cobwebs from their faces with their forefeet." In 1892, in Gainesville, Florida, "great white sheets," resembling "large, pure white spider webs, some of them fifty yards or more in length," drifted from the sky.

Although many published reports refer to this so-called angel hair as cobweblike in its appearance, few mention the presence of spiders. Yet spiders have doubtless been the cause, in particular one type of balloon spider that uses updrafts to migrate. It emits a globule of liquid silk from its abdomen that can be spun out many feet; as the breeze catches the thread, the spider is borne aloft and carried for miles. Landing, it releases the thread, which drifts off. When numerous spiders are involved in such migratory behavior, the air can become thick with the discarded filaments. □

An unidentified crystalline substance sweet as candy fell twice in Lake County, California, in September 1857. Several women used it to make syrup.

The Kentucky Meat Shower

Chunks of fresh red meat three to four inches square showered down over an area 100 yards long and 50 yards wide in Kentucky in 1876. To startled people on the ground, it looked like beef: Two men tasted it, and they identified the meat as either mutton or venison. A careful examination of seven samples revealed that it consisted of muscle, lung, and connective tissue. Locals pondered the meat shower and decided that the only possible solution to the mystery was a flight of well-fed buzzards, which, "as is their custom, seeing one of their companions disgorge himself, immediately followed suit." □

Frog Falls

Caught in a thunderstorm while working on a construction project in Bournemouth, England, a laborer witnessed a sight he would never forget: yellow frogs the size of half crowns falling with the rain. So numerous were they that many became impaled on the spines of gorse bushes in the nearby commons. For days afterward, the stench of dead frogs lingered in the air.

The incident, which took place in 1891, is but one of hundreds of accounts of falling frogs, toads, and tadpoles reported from around the world. The phenomenon is even mentioned in the Bible; the second plague of Egypt brought with it a mighty onslaught of airborne frogs.

Falls of toads seem to be commoner in some countries than those of frogs. France, for example, has had an outsize share of toad showers. Several hundred of the creatures landed among 150 men of the grand guard in Lelain, in 1794. An incredulous soldier, holding out the corners of his handkerchief, caught dozens of them in it. In 1833, toads bounced down on the town of Jouy near Versailles, landing on roofs and leaping off umbrellas onto the streets.

Greece is regularly visited by frog falls. One village in northern Greece, in fact, experienced two dense falls, one in 1963 and one in 1979. During the second episode, the frogs covered the road so thickly that they brought traffic to a standstill.

Although it has yet to be proven, such showers of amphibians, like those of fish, may be attributed to whirlwinds and waterspouts, which gather up the animals from their homes and transport them willy-nilly elsewhere. □

Fishy Phenomena

Fish have fallen from the sky for centuries—alive and dead, whole and in pieces, and ranging in size from less than an inch to a foot in length. Reports of fish falls go back as far as ancient Egypt and have come from countries as far-flung as India, Burma, France, Ecuador, and the United States.

A nineteenth-century Englishman told how, on February 9, 1859, he was getting ready to saw some wood, "when I was startled by something falling all over me—down my neck, on my head, and on my back. On putting my hand down my neck I was surprised to find there little fish. By this time I saw the whole ground covered with them. I took off my hat, the brim of which was full of them. They were jumping all about. My mates and I might have gathered bucketfuls of them, scraping with our

hands." That indeed is what some Singaporeans did when fish rained down in 1861; they filled their baskets with them and ate them. When fish fell on a British army in India in 1809, the general in charge did not let a good thing go to waste, either: He had some of them cooked for his table. And an Australian couple in 1989 *(above)* was similarly motivated when they swept up some of the fresh sardines that had landed on their property and fed them to their cat.

American fish falls have been numerous. A biologist for Louisiana's Department of Wildlife and Fisheries happened to be present when fish descended on the town of Marksville, in 1947. He told how hundreds of the creatures pelted residents and littered Main Street, where automobiles and trucks ran over them. He identified the fish as native to local waters.

More recently, in 1986, a fishing trawler plowing through the waters of Lake Michigan found itself under bombardment from smelts during a heavy storm. As if high waves and engine failure were not misery enough for the three-man crew, the tiny fish accumulated on deck in sufficient numbers to nearly capsize their vessel.

How such fish become airborne is a question that has been much discussed. The best guess is that they are swept up by tornadoes, whirlwinds, and waterspouts, and then released when the turbulence subsides. □

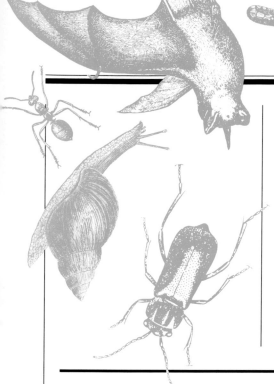

Horrid Creatures from the Sky

More than fish, frogs, and toads have fallen live from the sky. Snakes, snails, beetles, and ants have all made sudden, unexpected, and unwelcome appearances. In 1872, in Bucharest, Romania, citizens were horrified by a shower of black worms the size of houseflies. The grubs descended from a small cloud that had appeared overhead; before passing, it had discharged enough of the worms to blanket the streets. Jellyfish splattered the roads of Bath, England, in 1894. And sick and dying bats plopped onto Fort Worth, Texas, in 1989, sending residents scurrying for shelter.

The captain of a fishing boat sailing the waters off Wales in 1954 was surprised when a rat dropped from the clear blue sky onto the deck. After killing the rodent and tossing it overboard, he saw a sea gull swoop down for the carcass. Then he guessed what had happened: The rat had probably been the gull's prey, lost earlier when it squirmed from the bird's beak. □

Dead on Arrival

Birds may be masters of the air, but there have been occasions when thousands of them in midflight have suddenly plummeted to the earth—dead.

The largest recorded incident of this kind occurred at Warner Robins Air Force Base, south of Macon, Georgia, in October of 1954. The bodies of no less than 50,000 birds, representing fifty-three species, littered the runways. A few years later, on August 18, 1961, thousands of sooty shearwaters dropped like bricks along the coast of California from Pleasure Point to Rio Del Mar.

The causes of such mass kills vary. Some birds have been victims of lethal thunderclouds, thrust by the powerful winds to high altitudes where they were battered by turbulence and unable to breathe effectively. Apparently this was the case in 1978 when a flock of pink-footed geese got caught in an updraft over Norfolk, England, and then fell lifeless from the sky in a straight line stretching some twenty-eight miles across the countryside. Other birds have been struck by lightning while in flight. Still others have had their wings iced over, as happened to mallards above Stuttgart, Arkansas, in November, 1973. Unable to escape a hailstorm, the ducks came hurtling down, landing with a thud; they were frozen solid. □

This dead sooty shearwater is one of many that fell on Capitola, California, in August 1961, damaging cars and littering streets.

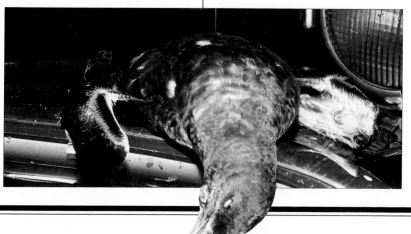

Heavenly Grit

Atmospheric researchers were baffled. Although they have long known that dust travels great distances in the upper atmosphere, they never counted on rock particles doing so as well.

In December 1988, a research team from the University of Rhode Island reported that quartz bits, between 50 and 200 micrometers in diameter, journeyed 6,000 miles from a dust storm in China to an area not far north of Hawaii—a trip that took a week.

Experts are not surprised when red dust, raised during droughts in North Africa, combines with moisture and comes down as red rain in Miami some 4,000 miles away. But particles as relatively large as the ones from China were always thought too heavy to make such a long trip. The only possible explanation seems to be that violent weather kept them aloft. □

Seeded Skies

Corn, peas, seeds, nuts, and fruit have all fallen from the sky, sometimes with painful consequences. In 1951, workers atop New York's Empire State Building had to take cover from a hail of stinging barley grain. In March 1977, Mr. and Mrs. Alfred Osborne of Bristol, England, were on their way home from church when they found themselves being pummeled by hazelnuts. The couple rejected the notion that a strong wind might have caused the shower, noting that the sky had been clear and the wind calm before the onslaught began. "Besides," Mrs. Osborne observed, "I don't know where you could find hazelnuts in March." And in November 1984, Mr. and Mrs. Derek Haythornwhite were wakened by thundering noises on the roof of their East Crescent, England, home. "When I looked out," said Mrs. Haythornwhite, "I thought they were giant hailstones. Then I rubbed my eyes and saw they were apples." Moreoever, they were apples of the best sort. According to Mrs. Haythornwhite, there had not even been an airplane in the sky. The apples continued falling for an hour. □

Trevor Williams holds a handful of peas—some of the thousands that pelted his home in Tonna, South Wales, in April 1980.

THE FIERY PLANET

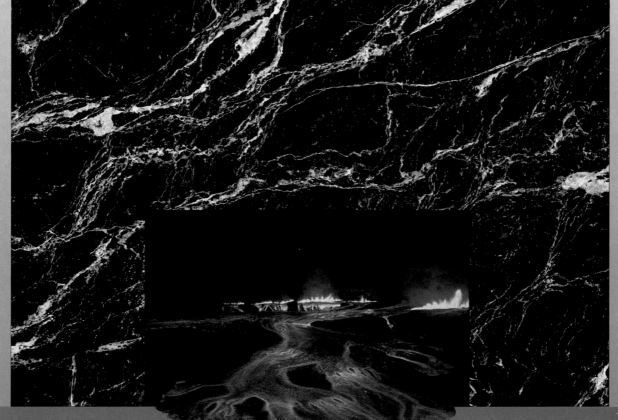

T ormented by fero-
cious heat during its birth
throes, the earth remains a fiery planet.
From on high, lightning from myriad thunderstorms lashes the globe almost constantly.
From deep within the earth, molten rock
bursts forth to build mountains, level cities,
and reshape continents. Often, vulcanism
strikes repetitive blows: Mount Tambora's
eruption in the early nineteenth century rattled the Indonesian island chain to its bedrock
and dimmed the daylight around the world; a
volcano on the nearby island of Krakatau thundered with kindred violence little more than a
half-century later.

Just below the Arctic Circle, volcanic Iceland grows today because the molten rock
beneath its surface
periodically bubbles and
spurts, raising a hill here, filling a valley there,
or creating an entirely new island in the sea
nearby. It is as if the land itself were sending
forth steaming colonies.

For all of their cataclysmic force, volcanic
eruptions can enrich the earth, promoting the
growth of lush vegetation. Throughout the
world, farmers and others are frequently drawn
to the fertile slopes of the most destructive
volcanoes. Indeed, some two million people
presently live hard by one of the deadliest of
mountains, Italy's famed Vesuvius. There they
draw nourishment from its soil and often mar-
vel at its beauty—and are all but heedless of
the sleeping fire below.

The Treachery of Vesuvius

Vesuvius, probably the world's best known volcano, is also the most persistently destructive. It has erupted at least fifty times in the last twenty centuries, killing tens of thousands of people and scouring entire villages from its flanks with blasts of gas and dust, rivers of mud, and massive, glowing flows of lava. And yet, again and again, new settlers—lured by the rich fertility of the volcanic soil and the sheer beauty of the setting on the Bay of Naples—have eagerly taken the places of the volcano's last victims.

The ancient Romans, who built the sparkling white resort cities of Pompeii, Herculaneum, and Stabiae at the mountain's foot and scattered their richly appointed villas on its slopes, refused even to believe that Vesuvius was a live volcano—despite tales of eruptions handed down from earlier Greek settlers. The mountain seemed too peaceful and bounteous to be a threat. Its fields yielded two or three grain crops a year; its orchards burst with figs, apples, pears, and cherries; its vineyards produced good wines. Even when an earthquake destroyed half of Pompeii and Herculaneum in AD 62, the Romans gave no thought to a volcanic cause. They did not hesitate to rebuild the cities, more grandly than before.

Then, in AD 79, an hour after noon on August 24, the mountain's top split open with a blast of thunder. An immense column of black smoke and ash rose, pierced by the fire of glowing cinders and lightning. Pliny the Younger, a Roman scholar whose account of the eruption marked the beginning of modern volcanology, said the ash column resembled a towering pine tree, with a high, straight trunk and a horizontal spread of branches at the top. This type of eruption—observed often throughout the world—is now called Plinian.

Ash, stones, and chunks of pumice rained down on the terrified residents of Pompeii. Nine miles away, a river of hot mud entombed Herculaneum. Vesuvius continued to erupt for eight days. Thousands left their homes and escaped destruction, but another 16,000 died—struck down by flying stones, suffocated beneath powdery ash, buried under mud, or killed by steam and poisonous gases that poured from the volcano. Pliny, fleeing with his mother, narrowly avoided such a fate at the hands of "a dense smoke, which came rolling in our track like a torrent."

Over the centuries that followed, Vesuvius erupted again and again.

An 1822 eruption of Vesuvius was captured in this contemporary watercolor painted by an anonymous artist.

In the year 472, ash from an eruption fell on Constantinople, 775 miles away. In 1538, the volcano threw out stones "larger than an ox." By 1631, cattle again grazed peacefully in the crater—until December of that year, when Vesuvius once more opened, spilling seven rivers of molten rock down its flanks and claiming 18,000 lives—its greatest toll ever.

Today Vesuvius looms over an urban region that comprises some 2 million people—more people than have ever before lived in close proximity to an active volcano. And the threat of Vesuvius still stands, engraved on a tablet by the viceroy of Naples following the dreadful eruption in 1631: "Sooner or later this mountain takes fire. But before this happens there are mutterings and roarings and earthquakes. Flee so long as you can. For soon the mountain will burst apart and bar the way for those who are slow to flee." □

Cooked Fish and a Small War

Sicily's Mount Etna—the largest volcano in Europe—has dealt death to residents of surrounding villages in many ways: Its hot steam and lava have burned them, and showers of ash have destroyed crops and caused famine. And, on the one occasion when Etna seemed to provide rare bounty, those who partook of the volcanic feast paid with their lives.

In 126 BC, a mass of molten lava plunged into the Ionian Sea near the town of Lipari. The waters boiled violently, cooking thousands of fish. When the fish washed ashore, according to one chronicler, numerous citizens of Lipari gorged themselves and were promptly afflicted with a fatal "distemper."

Centuries later, in 1169, the town of Catania was subjected to more conventional horrors—and far more devastation—when a major eruption of Mount Etna, accompanied by an earthquake, buried more than 15,000 residents under collapsed buildings. That explosion—the worst in twenty-three centuries of recorded eruptions at Etna—was rivaled only in 1669 when, with a roar that could be heard for fifty miles, the side of the mountain burst open and sent a two-mile-wide river of lava gushing out over fifty villages and towns, eventually killing as many as 100,000 people—and starting a local war.

Catania had prepared for such an eruption by building a sixty-foot-high wall between itself and the volcano. But as the lava stream approached—with the ruins of entire farms floating on the bubbling surface—it became evident that the wall would not be adequate.

Draped in wet cowhide to ◊

In this painting of the 1669 explosion of Sicily's Mount Etna, lava rushes from Nicolosi *(upper left)* into Catania *(foreground).*

protect themselves from the heat, a crew of Catanians diverted the flow by hacking through the crust of cooled lava that formed a kind of levee along the edges of the flow. Thus freed, the stream poured away from Catania—and straight for nearby Paterno. In defense of their newly threatened town, the people of Paterno armed themselves with swords and lances and drove the Catanians away from the gap they had created. The breach soon closed and the lava resumed its former course for Catania, where it cascaded over the wall and ravaged the city. Even today, masses of lava from the 1669 eruption block many of Catania's old streets. □

Quiet Explosion

The May 18, 1980, eruption of Washington State's Mount St. Helens propelled a horizontal blast of ash-filled steam and gas at up to 670 miles per hour, instantly snapping off six million trees and scattering them like straws over a 130,000-acre area. The blowdown took place in eerie near silence: Muted by the cloud of ash, dust, and fir needles, the noise—which under other conditions might have been heard a dozen miles away—carried a mere thirty feet. □

In a 1772 eruption, the entire top half of Java's 8,750-foot Mount Papandayan sank into a bubbling pool of lava, bearing with it forty villages and 3,000 people.

The World's Biggest Blast

On the evening of April 5, 1815, the people of colonial Batavia, on the island of Java, heard what sounded like cannon fire rolling over the Java Sea. Two ships set out to investigate but found no apparent source of the sound. Over the next few days, however, volcanic ash falling from the sky and a continued rumbling in the ground provided a hint of the sound's origins. Finally, travelers brought news from the island of Sumbawa, located more than 750 miles away, that the mountain called Tambora had exploded. It was the largest volcanic eruption since the end of the Ice Age.

Long assumed to be extinct, the 13,000-foot peak had for thousands of years suppressed under its placid, lushly vegetated surface a reservoir of molten rock. That April, the pent-up pressure was violently released. The explosion shook the entire 2,500-mile Indonesian island chain, immediately killing 10,000 inhabitants of Sumbawa and the surrounding islands; 82,000 more people died from the famine and disease that followed.

The effects of the explosion were felt around the world. Tambora ejected an estimated thirty-six cubic miles, or 170 billion tons, of volcanic debris into the earth's atmosphere. So dense was the cloud of ash that it darkened islands 300 miles away for three days. The dust created a stratospheric haze that filtered sunlight around the globe for years—making for spectacular orange sunsets as far as England—and robbed parts of Europe and North America of a summer *(pages 87-88)*. □

The Death of Mighty Krakatau

In July of 1883, tourists stopping at the tiny Indian Ocean island of Krakatau complained of a curious and unsettling sensation: As they stepped off their boats, the ground felt unpleasantly warm.

The strange phenomenon was only one of several ominous signs that a huge volcano on the island was shaking itself awake after two centuries of dormancy. For months, Krakatau had been sputtering, sending out an increasingly dense cloud of steam and soot that cast a smoky pall over the islands and ocean west of Java. By August, ship captains were nervously avoiding the island. A resident of nearby Batavia wrote uneasily that windows in the Indonesian colonial capital were cracking from subterreanean vibrations emanating from "that devilish volcano out there in the ocean."

Krakatau finally fulfilled its terrible promise in the hushed dawn hours of August 27, when it erupted with a blast that was heard 3,000 miles away in Madagascar—the loudest noise in recorded history. Although not quite heard around the world, the eruption affected every corner of the globe with atmospheric disturbances. So great was the blast that the pressure waves it created circled the globe six and a half times. A century later, scientists calculated that its force had reached 30,000 megatons—one million times greater than that of the atomic bomb that destroyed Hiroshima in World War II.

A steam cloud shot 25 miles into the sky, and several billion tons of rock launched skyward by the blast created a deadly hail of red-hot matter that killed hundreds of people. By far the worst toll in human life was taken by giant tsunamis, sea waves set in motion by the blast. The waves, ◊

Clouds of steam and ash billow from Krakatau in this photograph taken just three months before the volcano's final, deafening eruption in August 1883.

reaching heights of 175 feet, crushed the town of Tetlok Betong, 50 miles from Krakatau, and killed its 10,000 inhabitants. More than 300 other towns and villages were totally destroyed; in many, the entire population was simply swept into the sea. Speeding through the ocean at 400 miles per hour, the tsunamis engulfed the harbor at Calcutta nine hours later; in the opposite direction, they demol-

ished the harbor at Perth, Australia. Sea waves attributed to the explosion were recorded a week after the eruption. More than a year later, floating islands of Krakatau pumice were discovered 7,500 miles away, some bearing live crabs and other creatures.

For all of its force, the eruption of Krakatau was not as large as that of Mount Tambora sixty-eight years earlier. But Krakatau earned

instant celebrity: It was the first great volcanic event to occur after Asia was connected to Europe and North America by underwater telegraph cables, and details of its eruption and aftermath were instantly reported to a fascinated world. Thus Krakatau—rather than the more powerful Tambora—has lingered in the popular mind as the most stupendous eruption of modern times. □

A GOLDEN GOUT of lava from Hawaii's Kilauea volcano throws up billowing clouds of steam as it arcs into the sea in December 1989. The molten rock had been flowing through a conduit of hardened lava, which suddenly cracked open, releasing the stream. Located some twenty miles from the volcano's main crater, this rare gusher spurted for nearly five days before cooling lava sealed the opening.

Pitiless Pelée

At the turn of the century, the port city of St. Pierre on the island of Martinique was one of the most prosperous and romantic of all Caribbean communities. Its winding cobbled streets and pastel architecture led one delighted visitor to call it "the quaintest, queerest and the prettiest withal, among West Indian cities." St. Pierre's charms were enhanced by its setting, between a sparkling blue harbor and the lushly vegetated slopes of Pelée, a quiescent volcano.

St. Pierre's idyll began to unravel in April 1902, when Pelée returned to life and began throwing off showers of powdery ash that drifted onto the city like gray snow. Soon, residents were complaining of sore throats and difficulty breathing. Then, on May 5, a mass of boiling mud burst out of the mountain and rushed to the sea, carrying fifty-ton boulders as if they were pebbles and burying alive forty workers in a sugar mill that stood in the way.

Despite these signs of an imminent major eruption, the governor of Martinique insisted Pelée posed no danger to St. Pierre. To avert a mass exodus and ensuing panic, he sent 1,500 troops into the city to prevent anyone from leaving.

May 8 dawned bright and clear. A gentle breeze deflected the ash fall away from the city, and it appeared that the governor was right. Then, at 7:59 a.m., Pelée blew apart. "There was no warning," wrote an eyewitness aboard a ship in the harbor. "The side of the volcano was ripped out and there was hurled straight toward us a solid wall of flame. It sounded like a thousand cannons. The wave of

From a hill overlooking the destroyed city of St. Pierre, a visitor surveys the scorched ruins. Mount Pelée, the source of the destruction, is in the background.

fire was on us and over us like a flash of lightning. . . . The town vanished before our eyes."

Tightly corked at the top by a plug of semisolid lava, the mountain burst open on the flank directly facing St. Pierre. A glowing cloud of superheated gas roared over the city. The cloud contained little free oxygen (necessary for combustion) so at first St. Pierre scorched rather than burned. But the heat was so intense—more than 1,000 degrees Fahrenheit—that many objects were instantly carbonized. For humans, a single breath meant death.

After the cloud had passed and the supply of oxygen returned—a matter of less than a minute—the city burst into flame. Its destruction by a hurricane of fire and wind was complete.

Out of a city of 30,000 souls, only 2 men survived the holocaust. One was a shoemaker named Léon Compère-Léandre, who watched, stunned, as those around him died. The second survivor was twenty-five-year-old Auguste Ciparis, a murderer who was held in St. Pierre's prison. Ciparis, like Compère-Léandre, was hideously burned, but his life was spared by the hard conditions of his confinement—his tiny, thick-walled dungeon was so poorly ventilated that he was protected from the full effects of the searing heat.

Compère-Léandre faded into obscurity after the disaster. Ciparis, granted a pardon, spent the rest of his life displaying his awful scars in a circus sideshow as "the prisoner of St. Pierre." □

Photographed in 1944, a year after it sprouted from a cornfield, the Parícutin volcano had reached a height of more than a thousand feet.

A New Volcano

A number of villagers in Parícutin, Mexico, had long been fascinated by a place nearby, where the sunken ground was always warm and made curious noises. It seemed almost magical: Each year, local farmers filled in the depression, but it always resumed its original shape. Then, on February 20, 1943, the earth opened into an 80-foot-long crack, which began spewing ash and red-hot stone.

A volcano was born. In its first day, it grew to a height of 35 feet. By 1952, it had topped out at 1,353 feet, burying two towns in the process. □

Rivers of Lava

Iceland is a 39,000-square mile island that owes its existence to volcanic activity. The eruptions that built it began millions of years ago and continue today, subjecting Iceland to a major outbreak every six to seven years. Almost one-third of the world's output of lava since the year 1500 has flowed on Iceland.

The most devastating eruption occurred in June 1783, when the volcano known as Laki tore open a fifteen-mile-long fissure. From this split in the earth, lava poured into the Skaftá River, replacing water with molten rock that overflowed the river valley.

The effusions continued for nearly two months. Moving forward on a front nearly fifteen miles wide, the lava filled a large lake and two river valleys—one fifty miles long, the other forty miles—whose gorges were up to 600 feet deep. The heat melted vast quantities of glacial ice, flooding the land; the resulting steam contributed to torrential rainstorms and additional floods. By the following spring, one-fifth of Iceland's fifty thousand people, and three-quarters of the country's livestock, had perished, trapped by lava, drowned in the flooding, or poisoned by noxious vapors and ash-polluted pastures. □

An arc of lava spurts through a fissure *(right)* in the vast field of hardened basalt that was formed from an earlier flow in Krafla, Iceland *(above)*.

Lightning shoots through the ash-laden volcanic clouds above Surtsey, a small island created in 1963 by eruptions off Iceland.

Fast and Furious

Meteorologists estimate that lightning strikes the earth 100 times each second, releasing built-up electrical charges in the 2,000 thunderstorms that are lashing the earth at any given time. Each lightning stroke travels at a speed of 80,000 miles per second—nearly half the speed of light—generating temperatures as high as 50,000 degrees Fahrenheit. □

Le Petit Journal

UN SONNEUR DE CLOCHES FOUDROYÉ

The grim death of a French bell ringer, Pierre Boude, in 1910 was illustrated in a contemporary magazine.

Lethal Bells

Throughout Europe, church bells cast during the late Middle Ages bear the Latin legend *Fulgura frango*—"I break the lightning." The inscription reflects the medieval belief that the ringing of church bells at the approach of a storm would somehow avert a lightning strike.

The practice persisted into the eighteenth century, despite clear evidence that bell ringing could in fact be fatal—at least to the unfortunate bell ringers. Lightning regularly struck church steeples, usually the highest structures in town, and 103 bell ringers were killed in one thirty-three-year period in Germany alone. □

Lightning Fireworks

On August 18, 1769, a bolt of lightning struck an eighty-foot-high stone tower built into the medieval defensive walls around the town of Brescia, Italy. The tower, which served as the town's gunpowder magazine, contained seventy-eight tons of black powder, which exploded in a spectacular blast. Rescuers dug 308 bodies out of collapsed houses; 500 more people were injured. □

Unsafe Oaks

Scientific studies seem to support an old wives' tale that holds that oaks are the most dangerous trees in the forest during a thunder storm, while beeches are more likely to offer safe shelter. A survey of lightning strikes in a German forest in the late nineteenth century revealed that in one eleven-year period, lightning struck fifty-six oaks, twenty firs, and three pine trees without touching a single beech—even though 70 percent of the forest's trees were beeches. Later studies have shown that oaks are forty-five to sixty times more likely to be struck by lightning than beeches, probably because of the high moisture content present in oak trees. □

Lightning Pranks

Ordinarily, a lightning strike is no laughing matter. But folklore and scientific literature are filled with tales of bizarre effects that make it easy to understand why the ancients considered lightning a plaything—as well as a weapon—of the gods. The French astronomer Camille Flammarion, who died in 1925, was a collector of such tales. In one, a girl was jerked through the air and deposited unharmed on top of her sewing machine when her room was struck. In another, a building was hit twice during the same storm. The first bolt started a fire; the second set off an alarm bell, summoning help to extinguish it.

The sudden intense heat that lightning generates can make the air in fabric expand so violently that clothes are literally blown off a person's back, as were those of a workman in Ashford, England, in 1878. The man was stripped naked and badly burned. An opposite result was obtained in 1943 when, according to the National Safety Council, a soldier was sealed in his sleeping bag when lightning struck and welded the zipper shut.

In other bizarre events:

- A lightning bolt that hit a house in County Mayo, Ireland, shattered the shells of a basket of eggs but left the inner membranes intact.

- A bolt struck a windowpane, somehow excising an almost perfectly circular two-inch hole.

- Every other one of a stack of twelve dinner plates was shattered when a house in Iowa was struck by lightning. □

A Fatal Bolt

Scalp tingling and hair standing on end due to the electrically charged atmosphere around her, a visitor to California's Sequoia National Park grinned obligingly at the camera on August 20, 1975 *(below)*. Five minutes later, after she had walked away, the observation platform on which she had been standing was struck by a lightning bolt that killed one person and injured seven others. □

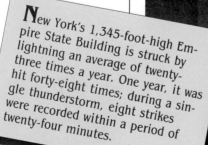

New York's 1,345-foot-high Empire State Building is struck by lightning an average of twenty-three times a year. One year, it was hit forty-eight times; during a single thunderstorm, eight strikes were recorded within a period of twenty-four minutes.

Fire in the Hills

When Sir John Franklin and his band of English adventurers sought a northwest passage through the arctic waters of Canada in the 1820s, they were confronted almost daily by new dangers and startling sights. But few experienc- es were more awesome and threatening than their encounter with the great clouds of acrid white smoke billowing from the cliffs of Cape Bathurst.

The rock and soil themselves were on fire, and the waters around

Photographed more than a century after their initial discovery, the burning hills of Canada's Cape Bathurst still smolder.

them were fouled with a sulfurous residue. Yet the wilted, half-frozen vegetation did not burn, and there was no evidence of volcanic activity in the area.

Franklin called the place the Smoking Hills and no doubt visited once again, two decades later, during his final—and fatal—expedition to the Northwest. The next recorded visitors were members of Captain Robert McClure's party, sent in search of the vanished Franklin in 1852. Sailors brought samples of the smoldering rock on board their ship—and watched them burn a hole in the captain's mahogany desk.

Naturally enough, the area had been long known to Eskimos, who dubbed it the "land of the sour ◊

water." Nineteenth-century whalers complained that the water wasn't fit for tea; indeed, ponds in the vicinity are as acidic as lemon juice. The smoke inhibits the growth of plants, and animals generally steer clear of the place. An exception is the herds of caribou who enter the acrid smoke for relief from the insect pests that plague them during the summer.

Judging from the extent of dead vegetation and charred cliffs, the Smoking Hills have been burning anywhere from several hundred to several thousand years. They are sparked by an exothermic reaction—one that produces great heat—between iron pyrite, buried sulfur, and bituminous shale, the same material that surrounds many coal deposits. The resulting fumes are as noxious as those from any coal-fired electric generating plant: They contain sulfur dioxide, sulfuric acid, and steam.

Spontaneous ignition of the soil occurs at a number of other sites around the world. At about the same time that Franklin arrived at Cape Bathurst, an Englishman noted smoke issuing from a seaside cliff near Weymouth; the rocks, when stirred, produced flames "of sufficient magnitude to allow of the toasting of a piece of bread." That fire burned for a few years but never covered more than fifty square feet. And early in this century, another Englishman reported smoking cliffs in the same vicinity. When he thrust a crowbar into the ground, a "bright, red-hot body of fire" was exposed. □

WORLDS OF ICE AND COLD

Among all the planets of the Solar System, Earth alone has moderate temperatures, which are suited to a huge range of life forms whose chief constituent is water. For most creatures—even those that are cold adapted—plunging temperatures can be disruptive or deadly. Frigid valleys in Antarctica are littered with the carcasses of seals that wandered too far from the more hospitable parts of the polar continent. And the shallow Norse graves along the shores of Greenland testify to the helplessness of human settlers against the so-called Little Ice Age that gripped the world in historic times. Even in lower latitudes, this chill era had life-altering effects, causing mountain glaciers to extend their icy tongues into green meadows and blanketing southern cities with snow.

For all that, severe cold has its fascination. The Little Ice Age gave Londoners a new playground—the frozen Thames River, upon which entire villages were erected for wintertime amusements. And today, thousands of people trek to the top of New Hampshire's Mount Washington each year to experience the bitterly chill winds that tourist brochures proudly promote as "the worst weather in the world."

Fairs on the Frozen Thames

In this painting from the seventeenth century, Londoners celebrate the freezing of the Thames River with a Frost Fair on the ice.

For more than 400 years, from the early fifteenth century to the middle of the nineteenth century, the so-called Little Ice Age held Europe in its grip. It was a time of especially short summers and cold winters that sent Alpine glaciers intruding into once-warm valleys and caused normally free-flowing waterways to freeze over.

In England, the broad Thames River froze frequently; Henry VIII is said to have traveled the frozen Thames from London to Greenwich by sleigh during the winter of 1536. Queen Elizabeth I took regular walks on the ice during the winter of 1564. That year, citizens celebrated New Year's Eve on the ice, and according to a contemporary account, "people, both men and women, went on the Thames in greater numbers than in anie street of the Citie of London." In January 1608, Londoners staged the first of many Frost Fairs on the river. Amusements included archery contests, ball games, dances, and bowling matches. Vendors set up booths from which they hawked food, beer, and wine.

The greatest Thames Frost Fair of all was held during the winter of 1683, when ice up to ten inches thick covered the river for two months. A second city was constructed. Formal streets were laid out, vendors and shopkeepers moved in, and as usual, all sorts of diversions could be found—among them bull baiting, horse and coach races, puppet plays, and much eating and drinking. An entire ox was roasted out on the ice. "It seem'd to be a bacchanalian triumph," wrote one eyewitness.

An enterprising printer by the name of Croom ran one of the fair's most popular attractions. For sixpence, Croom sold souvenir cards inscribed with his customer's name, the date, and the fact that the card was printed on the Thames River. It was estimated that he earned five pounds a day—an excellent living back then—selling the cards. One of his patrons was King Charles II.

The fairs were often brief—hastily established and dismantled at the whim of the weather. Frequently, rapid thaws resulted in the loss of property and life. One night in January 1789, the melting ice dragged at a ship moored to a riverside public house, pulling the house down and crushing five sleeping boarders.

The Frost Fair that began on February 1, 1814, ended just four days later and was as festive as all its predecessors. Blocks of ice, piled high by the river's current and tides, stood in stark contrast under the moonlight to the city's buildings. The usual games, races, and drinking were supplemented by the roasting of a sheep, and an elephant was led across the river below Blackfriars Bridge.

To celebrate the event, a printer by the name of Davis published a 124-page book entitled *Frostiana; Or a History of the River Thames in a Frozen State*. Davis finished printing his history on February 5, just hours before the ice cracked, sending shops, booths, and printing presses tumbling into the river. The Little Ice Age was on the wane, and London had seen its final Frost Fair. □

Greenland's Glaciers

When the Norse chieftain Erik the Red was exiled from Iceland near the end of the tenth century for committing murder, he traveled west to found new settlements on the verdant coast of a land he called Greenland. Over time, 3,000 colonists followed Erik, and farms began to spread over southwest Greenland. Sheep, goats, horses, and cattle thrived, and the fields were rich with grains.

Within three centuries, however, Greenland's fortunes began to change. The once-mild weather turned harsh; summers grew shorter and colder, crops dwindled, and livestock starved. The colonists became dependent on imported supplies. Finally, ice choked the seas and shut off Greenland from the outside world.

In 1492, the pope complained that Rome had received no word from the faithful of Greenland for eighty years. In fact, the last colonist had probably died, a victim of a period of global cooling now known as the Little Ice Age.

Today, a dome of ice as much as two miles thick covers more than three-quarters of Greenland—645,000 square miles—adding a burden so heavy that if it were lifted, the island's bedrock would rebound some 2,500 feet. Greenland's central ice sheet spreads in all directions. Outlet glaciers stretch their icy fingers through mountain passes, some pressing into fjords that once sheltered Erik's colonists. Among the most active of these is the Jakobshavn Glacier. Still flowing at the rate of 65 feet per day, its terminus spews 30 million tons of ice into the waters of its fjord every twenty-four hours. Together, Greenland's glaciers dump almost 20,000 icebergs into the sea each year. □

Cold Summer

In parts of Europe and North America, the year 1816 opened with a promise of peace and prosperity and concluded amid misery and unrest. In France, food riots triggered by crop failure added to the turmoil that followed the conclusion of the Napoleonic Wars. In America, a new wave of distressed New England farmers packed their belongings and joined the swelling westward migration.

Much of New England experienced snow in June and frosts in every month of that year. Unprecedented low temperatures were recorded from Virginia to Canada, earning 1816 a rueful name: Eighteen Hundred and Froze to Death. There were stretches of warm, seasonal weather that summer in New England, but a series of blasts of arctic air did terrible damage.

The first chill arrived overnight on June 5 and 6. At noon the temperature in Williamstown, Massachusetts, stood at eighty-three degrees. When citizens awoke the next morning it was forty-five degrees and falling. In Plymouth, Connecticut, it snowed for an hour on June 7, and clockmaker apprentice Chauncey Jerome walked to work in thick woolen clothes, an overcoat, and mittens. As far south as Virginia, killing frosts occurred nightly for several days. Tree leaves withered, birds froze to death, and shorn sheep perished. By the time the cold spell eased on June 11, most of the corn in New England had withered and died.

Good weather returned long enough to permit farmers with reserves of seed to replant their fields. Then, as the new sprouts began to flourish, the second cold wave arrived in July. Corn, beans, cucumbers, and squash were decimated; desperate New England farmers began talking of famine.

Their fears were real, and widespread food shortages were probably averted only by a brief warming that allowed hardier grains such as rye and wheat to survive. Then, on August 20, temperatures once again plunged, destroying the few remaining crops. And any hopes for a mercifully mild Indian summer were dashed a month later, on September 27, with the coming of another killing frost.

In northern Europe, the summer of 1816 was cool and wet. Farmers had hoped to rebuild reserves depleted by a decade of war; instead, food production was far below normal. Carts bearing wheat to market had to be escorted by soldiers to fend off hungry citizens. Switzerland's normally bustling grain market grew quiet, and farmers were forced to kill their swine because there was no grain for feed.

At the time, some scientists blamed the chill summer on sunspot activity, and one investigator theorized that the North Atlantic ⟩

had been overrun by arctic ice floes. And there were people who held that widespread use of lightning rods, invented in the 1700s by Benjamin Franklin, had somehow unbalanced a natural flow of warming electrical currents.

Not for nearly a century would anyone determine the true cause of the unseasonable cold spell. In 1913, a United States Weather Bureau scientist, William Humphreys, established a link between the frigid summer and a series of volcanic eruptions—most notably at Mount Tambora in the Dutch East Indies (now Indonesia). Blasting nearly 200 billion tons of ash high into the atmosphere, this epic explosion *(page 73)* created a pall of dust sufficient to block a significant portion of the sun's rays.

To be sure, Humphreys had not been the first to suggest such a possibility. More than thirty years before the Mount Tambora eruption, Benjamin Franklin had speculated about the connection between atmospheric dust and the weather. But in the cold summer of 1816, he was remembered more for his lightning rods than for his meteorological theories. □

Ice Islands of the Andes

Among the many wonders of the Andes highlands are huge, ghostly islands of ice that rise from the shallows of saltwater lakes. The most striking may be the ice islands of Bolivia's Lake Colorada *(right)*, which takes its name from the orange color of the plankton in its waters. The striped slabs of ice—their alternating layers of frozen fresh water and sediment laid down with craftsmanlike precision—tower more than twenty feet above the lake. Similar ice islands have been found in nine other Andean lakes in Bolivia and Chile.

Melted, the islands provide water pure enough to drink. Yet they rise from lakes that are saltier than the ocean. Their origins are uncertain. One theory holds that water from hot volcanic springs—uncontaminated by the lakes' brine—makes its way to the surface, where it freezes. Not all lakes with ice islands contain volcanic springs, however, leading some researchers to hold that the islands are remnants of a long-ago ice age. □

Glacial Speed

Glacial ice currently occupies 11 percent of the earth's land area, and "nature's ploughs," as glaciers are aptly dubbed, carve the terrain on every continent except Australia. In such places as Switzerland, they are largely curiosities and tourist attractions; in Greenland and Antarctica, their influence is so great that they shape the weather around them.

Glaciers form wherever snow accumulates faster than it can melt. Within days after they fall, snowflakes lose their delicate form and are compressed into granules, which eventually fuse together into huge ice crystals, some as large as soccer balls. To become a glacier, the frozen mass of crystals must accumulate to a critical thickness—about sixty feet; at that point, the weight of the ice causes an implacable downhill flow.

Although some glaciers barely creep, others slide along with surprising speed. Their rate of travel is determined by a mix of factors that includes ice temperature, steepness of the underlying ground, the bulk of the glacier, and the flow of water between the glacier and the underlying ground. The movements are not always predictable. In July 1966, for example, the Steele Glacier in Canada's Yukon Territory—a river of ice roughly the size of Manhattan Island—became known as the Galloping Glacier when it unexpectedly began spurting forward at the rate of two feet per hour. When it stopped a year later, it had traveled more than six miles, leaving no clues to the cause of its movement or its halt. □

In the late summer at Tierra del Fuego, at the southern tip of Chile, the tongue of Oblicuo Glacier reaches toward the Beagle Channel.

The Great White Hurricane

On Saturday, March 10, 1888, as the mildest winter in seventeen years was drawing to a close, New Yorkers thronged Manhattan's Central Park to enjoy yet another balmy weekend day. The temperature climbed into the fifties, and Elias B. Dunn, chief of the U.S. Signal Service's local weather observatory, expected only a few light showers to mar the rest of the weekend. At 9:30 that evening, Dunn telephoned the city's newspapers with his forecast for the following day: "cloudy, followed by light rain and clearing."

It was not to be. Sunday afternoon brought drenching rains, a furious wind, and plummeting temperatures. Dunn sought information from Signal Service headquarters in Washington—only to learn that all communication between New York and the outside world had been

severed; freezing rains had broken telephone and telegraph lines.

A giant mass of arctic air had roared into the New York area from the northwest, colliding with warm, moisture-laden air from the south and spawning furious storms all along the Eastern seaboard. Late on Sunday, the two systems joined forces over the Chesapeake Bay, producing heavy snow and hurricane-force winds that destroyed a hundred vessels within a few hours. As the storm raced toward New York, it became, in effect, a winter hurricane, filled with moisture and driven by cold, violent winds.

The city was completely unprepared for the

onslaught. When residents awoke on Monday, ten inches of snow were on the ground. More was falling, and ferocious winds were heaping it into towering drifts. The icy blast propelled broken signs, trash-can lids, and shards of glass from wind-shattered windows

A small crowd gathers on a Manhattan street (*above*) after New York City's devastating blizzard of 1888, and shopkeepers dig out their snowbound businesses (*left*).

along the streets like shrapnel.

The transportation system collapsed. Trains on all four of the city's elevated lines stalled, leaving 15,000 passengers stranded in unheated cars; trolleys were blown off their tracks and abandoned where they lay. And that was hardly the end of the jumble in the streets. As the New York *World* reported, "Great trucks piled with carcasses from the slaughter houses, broken down hacks, delivery wagons and overturned milk carts found place in this mournful display."

New Yorkers who tried to brave the storm on foot were knocked flat by the wind and enveloped in the driving snow; dozens were buried in drifts, their bodies only recovered days later. Saloons did a brisk business, as many city dwellers flocked to the nearest one to wait out the storm.

Meanwhile, at the weather station where Dunn and his staff were trying to make sense of the appalling conditions, the anemometer, its propeller jammed with ice, stopped taking measurements of the wind velocity. Dunn's deputy, Francis Long, inched his way up the mounting pole, swaying 175 feet above the street, and repaired the instrument—which went on to record gusts ranging from 75 to 100 miles per hour.

But no amount of data collected that day could take the full measure of the storm, one of the most ferocious and costly in United States history. By the time it blew itself out, the Great White Hurricane, as it became known, had blanketed the East coast from Maine to Maryland with more than twenty inches of snow, entombed houses in drifts as high as 52 feet, and taken 400 lives. □

Europe's Coldest Winter

As merciless as the barbarian invaders of the distant past, a blast of Siberian air swept over Europe in February 1956, subjecting the continent to the coldest, most ruinous winter of the century. No country was spared economic disaster and human misery.

Snow fell on Rome for six straight days, and 80 percent of Italy's citrus and olive trees died. In Spain, fifty thousand fruit pickers were left jobless as orange groves were frozen. Food prices skyrocketed with the loss of France's winter crop. Humble dandelion greens sold for almost a dollar a pound in Paris.

The Rhine froze, paralyzing vital river shipping and closing German factories for want of supplies. Burst water pipes flooded the homes of 10 million Britons. And even cold-inured Scandinavia was shaken by the ferocity of the weather. In one Swedish village, residents spent six days dynamiting themselves out from behind a massive snowbank.

Everywhere, wild animals were driven to desperate boldness by cold and lack of food. Hundreds of starving rats swarmed into a farmhouse outside Lausanne, Switzerland, and devoured virtually everything in sight, including the curtains at the windows. A woman in England discovered a fox in defiant possession of her hearth. And Polish villagers formed armed posses to fend off foraging wolf packs. A postman trapped in snow fifty miles outside Rome was reportedly eaten by wolves.

Before spring broke its cruel grip, the winter of 1956 had cost Europe two billion dollars in property damage and 907 lives. □

The World's Worst Weather

The 6,288-foot summit of New Hampshire's Mount Washington stands far below the peaks of the planet's highest mountains. But it also rises near the spot where three major storm pathways in the United States converge and thus makes up for its modest size by producing a combination of wind, snow, cold, cloud, and ice that some people have called the worst weather in the world.

The strongest wind ever to be measured on earth—231 miles per hour—was clocked on Mount Washington. At the peak, 250 inches of snow falls annually. The average year-round temperature is below freezing, and a layer of permanently frozen ground extends from a depth of about 20 feet down to 100 feet below the surface. Although it is possible to see five states, Canada, and the Atlantic Ocean from the top, the opportunity seldom arises: On average, cloud sheathes the summit at least part of 314 days a year.

The temperature at the peak is typically 15 to 20 degrees lower than in the surrounding valleys, although differentials of up to 45 degrees have been recorded. The mountain's official low temperature is 47 below zero Fahrenheit. At the summit, the cold combines with consistently high winds, producing wind-chill temperatures that sometimes exceed 150 degrees below zero Fahrenheit. On 1 out of 3 days from November to April, the winds reach 100 miles per hour or more. Clockings of more than 150 miles per hour are recorded nearly every winter.

To withstand such blasts, the original summit observatory was built in 1937 of nine-by-ten-inch railroad timbers, mortised to each other and bolted to the mountaintop. In 1980, a new steel-reinforced concrete structure with walls up to 2 feet thick was built into the peak.

The high winds join forces with Mount Washington's almost constant clouds to cloak the summit in sculptured layers of rime, a kind of ice that forms on contact when wind-driven clouds or fog strikes any solid object. Overnight, it builds feathery white coatings up to 3 feet thick on buildings, television towers, guy wires, and rock outcroppings.

As inhospitable as Mount Washington is, the mountain has fascinated people for centuries. The region's Indians are said to have called it Agiochook, the "place of the Great Spirit." Colonist Darby Field was seeking gems, not the spirit, when he became the first white man to ascend the mountain in 1642, but he returned empty-handed. By the 1860s, the mountain had become a tourist attraction, with a cog railway and carriage trail—later a toll road—carrying visitors to the top during the brief summer season.

Mount Washington's appeal has sometimes proven fatal. Since the first recorded death in 1851, nearly a hundred people have died on the mountain from falls, exposure, and simple inexperience with the capricious mountain weather. Perhaps the best known of all Mount Washington victims is Lizzie Bourne of Kennebunk, Maine, a member of a climbing party that began an ascent of the peak on September 14, 1855. Arriving at a rest stop called the Halfway House late in the afternoon, Lizzie and her companions disregarded the caretaker's advice to stay overnight and complete their climb in the morning. As the climbers continued upward, they encountered strong winds, freezing cold, and dense fog. Finally, exhausted and unable to continue, the party erected a stone windbreak and huddled together. Lizzie Bourne died at ten that night; in the morning, the survivors discovered that they had given up their struggle against the storm only a few hundred yards away from the Tip-Top House, an inn located at the mountain's windy summit.

Today Mount Washington's peak is occupied year-round by an intrepid, self-sufficient band of weather observers who report on meteorological conditions eight times daily—a task that brings them into regular contact with the worst of the mountain's elements. They also monitor scientific experiments, appear on live weather shows for local radio stations, write articles for the observatory's newsletter, and aid lost or injured hikers. Despite the isolation and hardship, the summit staffers have what one of their number has called "the highest paying job in the Northeast." □

Snowy Weapons

During World War I, soldiers fighting in the rugged outposts of the Tyrolean Alps were threatened by avalanches—both as a natural enemy and as a weapon wielded by human foes. On December 13, 1916, as many as ten thousand Austrian and Italian troops died in the worst natural avalanche disaster in history—more than one hundred snowslides that roared down the eastern slopes of the Alps, triggered by a brief thaw.

Soldiers on both sides put avalanches to offensive use. Gunners fired artillery rounds into snow-laden slopes in order to send avalanches crashing onto their enemies' heads. Between forty thousand and sixty thousand soldiers are believed to have been killed in these barrages; bodies of victims were still being discovered as late as the 1950s. □

According to legend, the Virgin Mary inspired Pope Liberius to erect a church at the site of a surprise summer snowstorm in fourth-century Rome. In this painting, the pope draws plans for the building in the snow.

Distant patches of snow dot the west end of Wright Valley, one of the few areas of Antarctica not buried beneath layers of ice and snow.

The Coldest Desert

Covered with ice averaging two miles thick, lashed by blizzards and blowing, blinding snow, Antarctica is the world's largest desert. On average, the continent receives the equivalent of just six inches of rainfall each year, only slightly more than the Sahara.

Antarctica remains the coldest continent, even though it receives more hours of sunlight each year than the warm equatorial regions. But sunlight falls on the equator from directly overhead, retaining its heat during a relatively short passage through the atmosphere; light reaches the poles at an oblique angle, passing a greater distance through the atmosphere and losing most of its heat energy. Antarctica is cooled further by its mantle of snow, which reflects more than 80 percent of the sun's energy back into space instead of absorbing the rays and thereby converting them to heat. □

Inside a Ping-Pong Ball

One of the most-feared hazards of Antarctic travel is whiteout, a weather condition that creates a world so confusing that one veteran of the Antarctic describes it as "wandering around inside a Ping-Pong ball." Whiteouts occur throughout the world, wherever snow covers large, flat areas. They can be caused by fog, blowing snow, or fine precipitation, but most often occur in clear, calm air under an unbroken layer of heavy, low-lying cloud that stretches from horizon to horizon. The uniform overcast diffuses the light and causes it to reflect between cloud and snow, obliterating all distinction between earth and sky.

Without the horizon to serve as a visual reference, it is nearly impossible to judge depth or distance; what appears to be an oil drum 100 yards away can turn out to be a soup can at arm's length. Shadows and surface details disappear. Small holes and large crevasses alike are indistinguishable from the surrounding snow, and a single step can result in a fatal fall. Vertigo is common, and its accompanying dizziness can make any movement dangerous. Whiteouts are especially hazardous to aviators who unwittingly fly into them while attempting to land.

Antarctic veterans long ago devised the only certain plan for whiteout survival, at least while on the ground: Sit down and wait it out. Sooner or later the light returns to normal, details of the landscape can be distinguished, and travel can resume. □

Colorful Icebergs

On March 22, 1971, while cautiously making their way through the frigid seas surrounding the South Orkney Islands near Antarctica, crew members aboard the British ship *John Biscoe* spied an extraordinary sight—a dozen icebergs striped and banded in black and green like a clutch of frozen exotic beasts. One berg, resembling a giant zebra, had more than twenty vertical stripes dividing its 100-yard length. Others were piebald, with broad bands and blotches of black and white.

These were dramatic examples of the variegated, colored icebergs that mariners occasionally encounter on polar seas. Unfortunately, the sightings have not yielded any clear explanations for the icebergs' colorations. Some dark bands—such as those of the *Biscoe*'s frozen zebras—seem attributable to layers of sediment that were embedded in the bergs' parent glacier. But much black ice is crystal clear—and no rocky debris can account for the magical blue and green ships of ice that sometimes sail in chill waters. □

Icebergs from Antarctica (*above*) and Greenland (*below*) display unusual colors imparted by minerals, sediment, and algae.

Hot Lakes and Mummified Seals

During the 1960s, American scientists drilled through the ice of Antarctica's Lake Vanda and found that the water below lay in four distinct layers—each saltier and warmer than the one above it. At the bottom, some two hundred feet beneath the frozen surface, the dirty, salt-saturated brine measured an astonishingly warm seventy-seven degrees Fahrenheit.

Lake Vanda is one of many saline lakes that lie in the so-called ice-free valleys of the Transantarctic Mountains. These lakes exist due to a set of unique conditions.

The lakes have no outlets and are fed by glacial meltwater streams carrying small amounts of salts and other minerals. Over hundreds of thousands of years, large quantities of these dissolved salts have accumulated in some of the lakes, settling in layers—the saltiest at the bottom because of lack of circulation. Paradoxically, the ice covering the lakes helps to warm them; vertical crystals in the ice conduct light into the depths, where it is absorbed by the dark, dense brine and generates warmth.

Among these lakes is "Mummy Pond," named for the mummified seals found along its shores. Apparently, they wandered in from the coast, sixteen miles away, then died in the harsh environment. □

A sheathing of ice covers the warm, salt water of Lake Vanda *(top)*. Scattered around this and other briny antarctic lakes are the mummified bodies of seals *(inset)*, some as old as 3,000 years.

Arctic Haze

In 1972, atmospheric physicist Glenn Shaw of the University of Alaska was asked to travel 300 miles north of the Arctic Circle to the little town of Barrow, on the Arctic Ocean, to measure the amount of dust in the air. Shaw viewed the trip as a waste of time. "Everyone," he wrote later, "knew that it was a very clean place." He was about to discover otherwise.

Shaw's first suspicions came before he even set foot in the north: When he peered from the airplane window, he could see a thick layer of haze blanketing the frozen land. Once on the ground, Shaw discovered that the sky looked white and milky, not deep blue as a clear sky should. Wielding a photometer, which gauges the absorption of sunlight by air-borne particles, Shaw concluded that the arctic atmosphere was not pristine, but polluted.

Shaw found few fellow scientists to accept his findings. One suggested that his photometer readings had been faulty; another explained that any particles in the air must be ice crystals. Over the following two years, however, Shaw continued to detect the presence of pollutants. Then, in 1976, a team of researchers from the University of Rhode Island began taking actual samples from the air in the Barrow area. Over the next few years, they confirmed the presence of unexpectedly high concentrations of vanadium, antimony, and other industrial by-products. Further analysis—including painstaking comparisons of arctic pollution with samples of air taken through-out the world—revealed that Barrow's wind-borne dirt originated in Europe and the Soviet Union.

By the early 1980s, the message was clear even to those who cherished the notion that arctic air is clean and pure: The pristine Arctic was a thing of the past. Each fall and winter, it seems, the seasonal currents of cold, dry air draw Europe's pollution toward the pole, where it mixes with water vapor to create the Arctic's thick haze.

So far, at least, the air at the South Pole remains pure—perhaps the cleanest air on earth. On a clear antarctic day, visibility can exceed 135 miles. The southern hemisphere contains relatively few sources of pollution, and its wind patterns do not sweep pollutants toward the pole. ☐

Unlike the hazy arctic region, Antarctica enjoys crystal-clear air, which makes distant objects, such as the mountains behind the penguins, appear much closer than they are.

A wall of ice cools a lava cave below the sun-parched surface of the desert near Grants, New Mexico. The size of the deposit has fluctuated over the years. It is shown here at a peak in the 1930s.

Unlikely Ice

Few regions seem less hospitable than the lava flows near Grants, New Mexico. The uneven ridges of sharp black rock flow across a parched, sunbaked land, unrelieved by streams or vegetation. Occasionally, cavelike depressions appear where the paper-thin crust collapsed into hollow bubbles formed by volcanic gases. At the bottom of these holes, the summertime temperature rises high above that of the surface. But one hole is different—blissfully cooled by air flowing from an adjacent ice-walled cave. The ice became a source of water and refreshment for early visitors; today it is a source of wonder to tourists.

The ice forms a solid deposit, some five feet high and forty feet across, that fills a cavity in what was once red-hot lava. When the lava cooled, it trapped bubbles of air that now serve as insulators.

The ice, tinted blue-green by airborne pollen, formed at a time when the region was far colder than it is today and is subtly striped with dust that settled on succeeding layers of freezing water. Although the air just outside this natural icebox can be witheringly hot, the ice melts only enough to produce a trickle of water. Winter rain and snow replenish the melting ice, although in recent years the deposit has slowly shrunk. □

WATERS OF LIFE

Water washes over three-quarters of the earth's surface, and its presence—or absence—defines the nature of life on the planet. The oceans' warm currents temper the climate of northern lands; rivers such as the Nile pierce otherwise inhospitable deserts, forcing bounty from the parched, miserly land. But the world's waters have a dark side, too: Rivers that give life can also destroy it in devastating floods; rogue ocean waves can wreck ships at sea and wipe out coastal settlements without warning.

Intriguingly, the lives of oceans, rivers, and virtually waterless deserts are woven together in geological history. Great seas such as the Mediterranean were once deep, dry plains crusted with the salty remainder of evaporated water. And many deserts that today are barren wastelands were once sea bottoms or lush plains nourished by networks of rivers.

6

Making a Big Splash

On a bright summer evening in 1958, the trawler *Sunmore* was plying the waters of Lituya Bay, a T-shaped inlet tucked among the mountains and glaciers of south-eastern Alaska. Suddenly, the twilight stillness was shattered; an earthquake shook the head of the bay, and 90 million tons of rock and ice plunged into the water from the northeast wall of the narrow Gilbert Inlet, which forms the left-hand arm of the T.

The resulting splash hit the opposite wall of Gilbert Inlet at a height of nearly 1,800 feet, and a wave 100 to 150 feet high raced at more than 100 miles per hour down the 7-mile length of the main bay. The *Sunmore*, which had been close to the shoreline near the splash, simply disappeared. Two other boats were in Lituya Bay at the time. One, the *Edrie*, was thrown into the center of the bay from its anchorage near the south shore; the second, the *Badger*, was lifted by the wave across a spit of land at the bay's mouth and into the ocean beyond, where it sank. The *Badger's* crew was rescued by a passing trawler.

Twenty-four hours later, the waters of Lituya Bay were quiet once more; the only sign of the previous evening's events was the floating bergs of ice—and a shoreline that had been stripped of soil and vegetation to a height of more than 100 feet. □

An arrow *(right)* marks the height of the splash—nearly 1,800 feet above sea level—caused when ice and rock, loosened from the opposing cliffs by an earthquake, crashed into Alaska's Lituya Bay. Further down the bay, the wave stripped trees from the shoreline *(above)*.

Killer Waves

On June 15, 1896, thousands of people gathered on the Sanriku coast, at the northeastern end of Japan's main island of Honshu. Caught up in the festivities of the Shinto holiday known as Boys' Festival, the revelers barely noticed several small shocks that trembled beneath their feet that evening. But an hour later a loud boom, followed by an eerie hiss, announced the catastrophe that followed. Before the stunned celebrants could react, the sea abruptly withdrew far from the shore, then rushed back in a seventy-five-foot-high wave—a tsunami, the most feared natural phenomenon in all disaster-prone Japan.

Although sometimes called tidal waves, tsunamis have nothing to do with the tides. They are triggered by seismic disturbances—coastal earthquakes, volcanic eruptions, or undersea landslides—that, in giving the ocean floor a jolt, turn it into something resembling a giant paddle. The water at the site of the disturbance gets what amounts to a big smack. The result is a deep wave that, unlike a surface wave, reaches all the way from the sea's surface to the floor and travels horizontally at speeds up to 500 miles per hour—as fast as a jet plane.

Despite its awesome power, this great pulse usually passes unnoticed beneath ships as it proceeds on its swift, sinister way through the ocean. Only as it approaches shore does the wave rise to reveal itself as a towering killer. The sharp elevation of the ocean floor near landfall acts like a brake on the bottom of the wave, causing vast quantities of water to pile up into a sheer wall, 100 feet or more high, that finally crashes onto shore with crushing force.

Often—though not always—the approach of a tsunami is signaled when the deep trough of the advancing wave causes the coastal waters to retreat as they did in Sanriku. Those who venture onto the dramatically bared beaches inevitably become victims.

The wave that struck Sanriku that day in 1896—the result of an offshore earthquake—was a textbook example of a tsunami. Fishermen twenty miles at sea had no awareness of the monster wave racing beneath their boats and were totally unprepared for the devastation that greeted them on their return to port through waters filled with wreckage and corpses. The giant wave had scoured 170 miles of coastline, swept up whole villages, and killed more than 28,000 people—drowned, crushed by falling buildings, or impaled on debris driven by the relentless wall of water. □

Triggered by shock waves from a deep-ocean earthquake *(arrow)*, a tsunami races across the sea at up to 500 miles per hour. Near land, the rising seafloor slows the advancing wave, causing the water to pile up to enormous heights as it crashes onto the shore.

Voyage to Hell

The earthquake that destroyed the port of Arica on the Peru-Chile border in 1868 presented a horrific sample of the deadly power of an earthquake and the resulting tsunami. Lieutenant L. G. Billings, an officer of the U.S.S. *Wateree,* later penned a vivid account of what it feels like to live through those twin agents of destruction.

The *Wateree* was anchored off Arica on the afternoon of August 8, when, with a frightful trembling, a huge dust cloud enveloped the city. When the dust cleared, Billings rubbed his eyes and gaped: "Where a few seconds before there had stood a happy and prosperous city, busy, active, and full of life, we saw nothing but ruins."

Responding to the cries for help from survivors crowded onto a jetty, the *Wateree* had just launched a small rescue boat when a giant wave broke, scouring the shore. Both those on shore and the thirteen crew members in the rescue vessel were lost. As is typical of tsunamis, the wave had passed unnoticed beneath the boats in the harbor. "Where a moment before there had been the jetty, all black with human beings, there was nothing: everything had been swallowed in a moment," wrote Billings.

At that instant another shock hit. This time, the sea drew back, only just setting the *Wateree* on bare sand before a second tsunami rushed in. The ship was lifted like a cork, Billings wrote. "From that moment on the sea seemed to defy all natural laws."

The *Wateree* was tossed around like a leaf by conflicting currents. When the turbulence subsided, the dazed crewmen lifted their heads and gazed into the eyes of a macabre audience: On the mountain above the ruined city, the earthquake had uncovered hundreds of centuries-old tombs. The occupants had been buried upright, and so the dead stood in ranks, as if in an amphitheater facing the sea and the hapless ship. Wrote the appalled Billings: "We were ready to believe that the Day of Judgement had come."

Merciful darkness soon blotted out the dreadful sight—only to bring a far more terrifying one: a third tsunami. "Staring into the night we first made out a thin phosphorescent line which, like a strange kind of mirage, seemed to be rising higher and higher in the air; its crest, topped by the baleful light of that phosphorescent glitter, showed frightful masses of black water below," Billings wrote. "Of all the horrors, this seemed the worst. We were chained to the bed of the sea, powerless to escape; . . . we could do nothing but watch this monstrous wave approach."

Then the sea was on them. "With a terrifying din, our ship was engulfed, buried under a half-liquid, half-solid mass of sand and water. We stayed under for a suffocating eternity; then, groaning in all her timbers, our solid old *Wateree* pushed her way to the surface, with her gasping crew still hanging on to the rails."

The next dawn's light revealed that the wave had carried the *Wateree* and two merchant ships over the shore, across a valley, and beyond a railway, two miles inland. Miraculously, all of the *Wateree's* remaining crew lived. But of Arica's 15,000 inhabitants, only a few hundred survived. "The town itself had disappeared: where it had stood stretched an even plain of sand." □

The Mighty Maelstrom

Nicholas de Lynna, a Franciscan friar who sailed into the polar seas from England in the fourteenth century, may have been the first foreign traveler to encounter Norway's Maelstrom, a whirlpool now so renowned for its danger to mariners that its name has become the generic term for all whirlpools.

Although similar, equally treacherous waters threaten mariners in the Strait of Messina between Italy and Sicily and in Japan's Naruto Strait, it is Norway's Maelstrom that remains lodged in fearful imagination. The most famous fictional account of the Maelstrom appeared in Edgar Allan Poe's short story "A Descent into the Maelstrom." In the story, a miscalculation of the tides and an unexpected storm trap three fishermen in a narrow passage, where the whirling of the waters intensifies until "the boat appeared to be hanging, as if by magic, midway down, upon the interior surface of a funnel vast in circumference, prodigious in depth."

Beneath its exaggeration, Poe's fictional account contains a remarkably accurate description of the forces that churn the Maelstrom into action. In the narrow strip of water between the islands of Moskenesoy and Mosken, the seafloor rises sharply, constricting the flow of the tide, with the result that a fresh, rising tide frequently begins its inward rush before the previous tide has finished its outward flow. The conflicting waters, further channeled by a jumbled, rocky seafloor, are whirled and spun into a confused mass. □

Watery Twisters

When John Caldwell saw a column of water whirling upward from the surface of the mid-Pacific on a July morning in 1946, he ignored the well-known observations of more seasoned sailors—that oceanic waterspouts contain hurricane-force gusts and voracious vortexes—and steered his vessel, the *Pagan*, directly into the spinning winds.

Soon, he wrote, "Pagan was swallowed by a cold wet fog and whirring wind. The decks tilted; . . . the rigging howled. . . . Suddenly it was dark as night. . . . I breathed wet air, and the hard cold wind wet me through. . . . I sailed into a high dark column from 75 to 100 feet wide, inside of which was a damp circular wind of thirty knots. . . . As suddenly as I had entered the waterspout I rode out into bright free air. The high dark wall of singing wind ran away."

Caldwell was fortunate to complete his encounter unscathed, for waterspouts can be as damaging as their feared landlubber cousins, tornadoes. On May 8, 1980, a funnel descended from a cloud, ripped the cabin off a shrimp boat in San Antonio Bay, Texas, sank the boat, and killed one of the three crewmen.

More benign are fair-weather waterspouts that form, as their name implies, in clear tropical air when temperature and humidity are high. Fair weather or foul, waterspouts reach high into the sky: The tallest ever recorded—at an estimated 5,014 feet—was seen May 16, 1898, off Eden in New South Wales, Australia. □

TERRIFIED RESIDENTS of Hilo, Hawaii, run for their lives from a 490-mile-per-hour tsunami created by an earthquake near Alaska, 2,300 miles away, on April 1, 1946. In the minutes before the wave struck, the sea level fell, luring many out onto newly bared reefs. It was a deadly trap: 159 were killed.

A tidal bore advances up the Tsien Tang River in eastern China.

A Boring Tide

Under a peaceful full moon, a nineteenth-century sailor on a ship near the mouth of the Amazon was startled out of his reverie by a rumble that sounded like distant thunder. Looking into the distance, he was horrified to see a broad, white wave of water fast approaching his vessel, "until it seemed as if the whole ocean had risen up and was coming, charging and thundering down." The sailor and his ship had encountered the powerful Amazon River tidal bore, the pororoca, a solitary wave that can reach a height of fifteen feet as it rushes upstream against the current at speeds of up to fifteen miles per hour, temporarily reversing the flow of South America's greatest river.

Tidal bores occur in some sixty wide, shallow river estuaries throughout the world at periods of exceptionally high tides. Where the underwater topography is most favorable, as it is at the mouth of the Amazon, a bore rises twice a day with the high tide, on the three or four days each month when the new and full moons exert their greatest pull on the tides. The bore's wall of water is raised when the incoming tide is pushed higher still by the shallow river bottom and then surges over the opposing current.

As it travels upriver, a bore's swell may be no higher than a few inches. But the angry churn of a crested bore can be high enough to overturn boats, flood riverside buildings, and uproot tall trees. More entertaining is England's Severn River bore, on which surfers ride upstream for miles.

The most unusual variation of a tidal bore occurs not at the mouth of a river, but on the broad, sandy tidal flats that stretch for miles between low- and high-tide marks at Mont-St.-Michel, off the northwest coast of France. At times, the rising sea races across the sand in one well-defined wave faster than a horse can gallop. □

When Water Falls under Water

Far from being placid pools, the earth's oceans are constantly in motion. Tides and currents scour the coasts, and huge cataracts fall for miles within the deep, dwarfing the waterfalls on the surface.

Seven major cataracts are found deep below the surface of the oceans. Most are driven by temperature differences between ocean basins: Heavy, cold water at the North and South Poles sinks to the seafloor, where it is channeled by the undersea terrain. Flowing downhill—deeper and deeper—the river finally plunges over a sill into an adjacent ocean basin.

The largest cataract is below the Denmark Strait between Greenland and Iceland. This submarine waterfall has a drop of nearly 11,500 feet—more than three times that of Venezuela's 3,212-foot Angel Falls, the highest waterfall on earth. Moreover, it carries at least 175 million cubic feet of water per second, making it 350 times as voluminous as Guaira Falls, on the border of Brazil and Paraguay, which—before it was submerged in the lake formed by a dam project—was considered to carry more water than any other falls on the surface. □

The Grandest Canyons

The floors of the earth's oceans, far from the reach of human eyes, are slashed and heaped in a rugged landscape that mirrors and magnifies the terrain above the sea. Under miles of water, mountains soar and chasms plunge to depths that dwarf dry land's most famous cut, the Grand Canyon of the Colorado River.

Perhaps the grandest canyons of all pierce the continental shelf beneath the icy Bering Sea between Siberia and Alaska. This is a land of submarine superlatives:

seven canyons clustered together, among them the 240-mile-long Bering Canyon, the 60-mile-wide Navarin Canyon, and the 9,000-foot-deep Zhemchug Canyon. In contrast, the Grand Canyon of the Colorado is only 10 miles wide and a mile deep, stretching 250 miles through Arizona.

The stage for the creation of the Bering Sea canyons was set some 75 million years ago, when slow movement of the vast plates that form the earth's crust created a broad shelf 8,500 feet above the deep ocean floor extending from Alaska to Siberia.

Although the shelf today forms the bed of the shallow northern half of the Bering Sea, it has often been exposed as dry land—most recently about 18,000 years ago when the last great ice age lowered the level of the oceans by about 400 feet. Scientists theorize that during these dry-land periods, the edge of the shelf began to crack and erode. Rivers flowing across the plain also cut into the exposed Bering Sea floor and deposited billions of tons of sediment at the outer edge of the shelf.

When the sea level rose, the forces of ocean waves and currents were loosed on shallow seafloor. The gullies in the shelf's edge widened; storm waves weakened the sediments, and gigantic landslides and mudflows—the major engines of the canyons' creation—swept down the steep slopes. In all, some 1,400 cubic miles of sediment and rock were thus removed in the creation of the Zhemchug Canyon. □

Underwater Smokestacks

Beneath the oceans, towering volcanic mountains stretch around the earth, pushing apart the vast plates that form the planet's surface. Throughout this vast mountain range, at an average depth of 8,200 feet, the ridge is pierced by rifts—vents that spew forth mineral-rich water at temperatures as high as 700 degrees Farenheit.

Off the west coast of Mexico, a mile and a half beneath the surface of the Pacific Ocean, these thermal vents take the shape of chimneys 10 to 20 feet tall, clustered on the ocean floor, spewing columns of black and white smoke like industrial stacks. Far from being a pollutant, this outpouring is an intensely hot solution of dissolved minerals that helps enrich the earth's surface and feed a menagerie of creatures peculiarly adapted to the conditions around the vents.

In the cooler, nutrient-rich waters near the vents, bacteria—not plants, as on the surface—form the basis of the food chain, drawing life from a chemical feast. Larger animals throng the vicinity; feeding on the bacteria and each other, they grow to amazing size. Red-tipped tube worms—looking like giant lipsticks—grow 6 feet long by absorbing organic material from the water, and foot-long clams reach maturity 500 times as fast as their relatives living in more conventional waters. □

Far below the surface of the Pacific, giant tubeworms (lower photo at right) grow in the hot, mineral-rich waters spewing from "black smokers," (upper right), aptly named thermal vents that often look like industrial stacks.

The Sources of the Nile

At 4,160 miles, the Nile is the longest river in the world. But although it gives life to much of the African continent, its full extent—and true source—were not found until almost the middle of the twentieth century.

From Khartoum in the Sudan, the river flows almost 2,000 miles north to the Mediterranean in a single stream formed by the confluence of the Blue Nile and the White Nile, each a major river in its own right. In 1615, the shorter Blue Nile was tracked to its source in Lake Tana, Ethiopia, 1,000 miles from Khartoum. Thereafter, the origins of the White Nile became the holy grail of adventurers seeking fortune and a place in history.

Most failed, although their probing of Africa's interior led to many other discoveries, among them Lakes Tanganyika and Victoria in 1857. It was in 1875 that British explorer Henry Morton Stanley determined that the Nile is Victoria's major outlet and that the lake has but one sizable inlet—the Kagera.

Nineteen miles from its source at Ethiopia's Lake Tana, the Blue Nile thunders over Tisisat Falls on its way to the desert of the Sudan, where it joins with the White Nile at Khartoum to form the world's longest river.

The source of that river, he reasoned, must be the source of the Nile. However, it was not Stanley but a lone, impoverished German explorer, Burkhart Waldecker, who finally traced the Kagera 250 miles to a mountainside in what is now Burundi. There, in 1937, he gazed upon the source of the mightiest river on the planet—ten tiny springs trickling into a ravine. □

River of Sorrow

The gritty burden of yellow sediment that gives China's Hwang Ho River its popular name—Yellow River—has also been responsible for a more sinister appellation: China's Sorrow.

Each year more than one billion cubic yards of sand and clay wash down the Hwang Ho's three thousand miles—six times the amount of earth that was excavated to create the Panama Canal. For thousands of years, as the stream slowed on reaching northern China's Great Plain, the silt settled, raising the riverbed and forcing the waters to spread wider across the flatland—most disastrously in times of flood. But beginning more than 2,000 years ago, the Hwang Ho has been channeled by levees to control flooding that to-

day carry it fifteen to thirty feet above the surrounding land.

Despite the levees, the waters frequently break through the dikes or cascade over them when swollen by the heavy rains of late summer, causing vast floods. In September and October 1887, for example, the River of Sorrow inundated 50,000 square miles, destroyed 300 villages, and by some estimates, killed up to 2.5 million people—the most devastating flood in recorded history.

Ironically, most of the river's victims have been peasant farmers, whose livelihood depends on the very circumstances that threaten them: The sediments left by flooding have made the Great Plain one of the world's most productive regions. □

In the Yangtze River flood of 1871, the waters rose so high that a river steamer snagged on a rock during the deluge found itself stranded 120 feet in the air when the water receded.

The Silence of Niagara

In the predawn hours of March 29, 1848, people living near Niagara Falls were awakened by an uncomfortable, eerie silence. The constant, thunderous roar of the falls had been stilled.

Hundreds of curious and frightened residents rushed to the banks of the Niagara River, the thirty-four-mile-long waterway that flows from Lake Erie into Lake Ontario, dividing Canada and the United States and feeding the mighty falls. A torchlight inspection revealed that the river had simply ceased to flow. "Far up from the head of Goat Island and out into the Canadian rapids, and from the foot of Goat Island out beyond the old Tower to the deep channel of the Horseshoe Falls, the water was gone," one witness reported.

Thousands of sightseers swarmed to the riverbank to gape at the empty channel and dry cliffs that remained. Some ventured into the streambed to seek out suitable relics of the occasion. Many others, sure the end of the world was at hand, rushed to churches on both sides of the border, where special services were held to forestall that evil.

Soon, the cause of the event was discovered. At the point where Lake Erie empties into the river, tons of lake ice had been piled by wind, waves, and currents, forming a solid dam that stopped the flow into the river. Two nights after it ceased, the Niagara resumed flowing. The ice dam disintegrated, and with a growl that grew to a roar, a wall of water surged and spilled over the great cliff. □

The Killer Lakes

Early in the morning hours of August 16, 1984, a group of people riding in a van with their parish priest approached the shore of Lake Monoun in the United Republic of Cameroon. Suddenly, the van's headlights picked out the figure of a man who appeared to be sleeping on his motorcycle. But when they stopped to offer help, the man proved to be dead.

Moments later, the priest collapsed, followed shortly by others in the party. Only one of the group, a young man named Foubouh Jean, escaped the mysterious malady. By midmorning, thirty-seven lifeless bodies had been found near the lakeshore—apparent victims of a vile-smelling chemical cloud that had drifted up out of the normally placid lake.

On August 21, 1986—two years later and fifty-seven miles away—loud, rumbling sounds issued from Cameroon's Lake Nyos, drawing a crowd of curious villagers. Soon, the lake belched up a white cloud smelling like rotten eggs, accompanied by a bubbling sound and a huge wave. As the cloud enveloped them, the witnesses were overcome by a warm sensation, and they lost consciousness. A few awoke, weak and confused, as much as thirty-six hours later.

Most never regained consciousness. More than 1,700 people died that night near Lake Nyos. Birds, cattle, wild animals, and insects also fell, and vegetation along the lakeshore was damaged.

The fatal clouds were apparently composed of carbon dioxide, a heavy, inert gas that asphyxiated the victims. But the origins of the gas remain uncertain.

Because the lakes occupy volcanic craters, some scientists theorize that volcanic gases rushed upward and surged over the lakes' rims. Most researchers, though, hold that the carbon dioxide had slowly seeped into the lakes and remained trapped in the cold water at the bottom. The gas was then released by a "turnover" of lake waters—a normal seasonal event in which cooling surface water sinks to the bottom, and warm water and gases rise to the top.

One piece of circumstantial evidence exists to support this latter theory: the release of both killing clouds in August, the month in which monsoon clouds bring cool weather to Cameroon's mountains and, presumably, a cooling turnover of lake water. □

Nature's Showmen

With wondrous regularity, Old Faithful, Yellowstone National Park's famous geyser, spews forth a 130-foot column of hot water and steam for as long as five minutes virtually every hour. But as geysers go, Old Faithful *(below)* is simply a squirt—even among its Yellow- stone neighbors. Yellowstone's Steamboat Geyser has erupted to heights of 380 feet, making it the reigning world champion, although Steamboat was once dwarfed by the Waimangu Geyser in New Zealand, which spurted briefly to 1,500 feet in 1904.

Geysers and their frequent companions, hot springs, are most often found in areas of volcanic activity. They develop when groundwater seeps deep into the interior of the earth, where it is heated by hot gases and molten rock, then trapped before it can make its way back to the surface. While the water remains trapped, pressure builds—finally becoming so great that a column of steam and water erupts through cracks in the earth.

Geysers take their name from a hot spring in southwestern Iceland—its name, Geysir, means "gusher" in Icelandic—which, when Norse settlers first arrived in the Middle Ages, erupted three times daily. It became inactive following a nearby volcanic eruption in the early twentieth century. Unlike Yellowstone's Old Faithful, most geysers are irregular performers, their eruptions depending on changes in the flow of underground water, the barometric pressure at the surface, and even the pull of the tides.

In many parts of the world, however, the showmanship of geysers is distinctly secondary to the energy they release. In Iceland the Geysir spring is tapped to help heat the city of Reykjavík. And at a place called The Geysers in northern California, steam issuing from the earth is harnessed to generate enough electricity to power a city of one million. □

A blue hole pierces
the Caribbean Sea
floor near South
Caicos Island in the
Bahamas.

The Blue Holes of the Bahamas

Sailors in the shallow waters surrounding the Bahama Islands, southeast of Florida, are often startled to see the white, sandy seafloor drop away, apparently disappearing in a dark blue pool. Sometimes hundreds of feet deep, these blue holes are actually subterranean caverns formed about 18,000 years ago, when a giant continental icecap removed oceanic waters, lowering the level of the seas by hundreds of feet.

At that time, the Bahama Islands were hills on a vast tropical plain. Rainwater, made acid by tropical vegetation, seeped into the soil, eroding and dissolving the limestone bedrock and creating vast subterranean caverns.

Some of the caverns collapsed under the weight of the surface soil, becoming sinkholes of the sort that dot the Caribbean landscape and that of nearby Florida. When the ice melted, the seas rose and submerged the lowlands; the sinkholes became the blue holes that would later inspire such fear and fascination.

Island fishermen know the holes as the legendary lair of the *lusca*, an octopus-like monster that emerges when hungry, roiling the waters with its arms and dragging boats and their crews to the bottom. Indeed, blue holes can devour boats, although no monsters lurk inside. The caverns trap the tidal flow within their underwater passageways, creating swift currents that churn the surface and form whirlpools capable of sucking small boats to the bottom. Divers, too, are vulnerable to the strong currents; usually the holes can be explored safely only twice a day, during the brief period when the tide is slack and the caverns' interiors are calm.

Once inside, divers find that blue holes enclose a fantasy world of rock and wildlife. Stalactites hang from the cavern roofs, relics of the time before the caverns were submerged; blind, colorless fish swim in their depths; lobsters and other crustaceans are abundant; and many species live nowhere else but in these marine caves. □

A HOUSE TUMBLES over a dam near Austin during a flash flood of Texas's Colorado River in 1935. Flash floods kill more people in the United States than any other natural disaster, and they damage more than one billion dollars worth of property each year.

Mediterranean Desert

Like many of the world's other seabeds, the bottom of the Mediterranean Sea was once dry land. Evidence shows that the ancient Mediterranean began drying up about six million years ago, creating a desert lying 10,000 feet lower than the surface of the Atlantic Ocean.

The sea kept its secret until 1970, when the ancient desert floor was breached by the deep-sea drilling ship *Glomar Challenger,* which retrieved 1,000-foot-long cores that provided a cross section of the seabed 10,000 feet below the surface. The cores revealed domes of salt and layers of sedimentary rock that could only have

been formed during the evaporation of an earlier sea. Gravel beds—rare in the deep ocean—furnished hints that the watery deeps were once hot, dry valleys and that islands such as Cyprus and Sicily were towering peaks.

The *Challenger's* evidence, described as scant but certain, was supported by coincidental discoveries in Europe and Egypt. France's Rhone River, which empties into the Mediterranean midway between Spain and Italy, and the Nile River—at the eastern end of the sea—were both found to have ancient gorges far below their present channels, so deep that the

rivers could once have watered grassy plains at the edge of a Mediterranean desert.

Geologists think the Mediterranean dried up when ranges of mountains were pushed up by forces within the earth, erecting a barrier that prevented the waters of the Atlantic Ocean from flowing into the sea.

The dam was breached at today's Strait of Gibraltar about five million years ago. Gushing through the gap at a rate of 10,000 cubic miles per year, the resulting falls would have dwarfed any present-day cataracts—and still required a century to fill the sea. □

Foggy Deserts

Although they lie next to the ocean and are blanketed in fog for part of each year, the coastal desert of western South America and the Namib of southwest Africa remain among the driest deserts in the world. The fog forms over the ocean when cold currents saturate the air with moisture. Onshore winds carry the fog over the desert, where it eventually burns away in the sun. However, the dome of high pressure that is responsible for the desert's heat and aridity remains stubbornly in place on the surface, preventing the formation of rain clouds. ⊔

Desert Rains

Portions of Chile's Atacama Desert on the west coast of South America have not received any measurable rainfall in fifty years. Parts of the Namib Desert in southwest Africa, though often foggy, receive less than one-fifth of an inch of rain each year. And Death Valley, the driest spot in North America, receives an average of less than two inches of rain annually.

However, when rains do fall on the desert, they are violent and destructive, slashing the parched terrain with deep erosion scars that are, paradoxically, a result of the desert's very dryness. Principally, the aridity retards the growth of vegetation that might otherwise absorb rainwater. In a matter of moments after a rainfall, sandy gulches called arroyos surge with muddy water. Sometimes floods overflow the steep arroyo banks and spread like viscous sheets, driving loose soil and boulders before them. One such flash flood in the Mojave Desert of California picked up a railroad locomotive and carried it for a mile before burying it in mud.

And then, as suddenly as they arise, the desert floods subside. The water evaporates in the sun and soaks into the soil, leaving behind an altered landscape that will only be changed again by the next downpour. □

Pierced by the peaks of the lower Andes, dense fog shrouds the coastal desert of Peru.

The Once Lush Sahara

In November 1981, when the United States space shuttle *Columbia* returned from its second mission, crew members brought with them remarkable radar images of the eastern Sahara. The pictures photographically peeled back the surface of the Selima Sand Sheet— a vast 39,000-square-mile plain where the sand lies up to 30 feet deep—and revealed the Sahara as it was some 10 to 20 million years ago: a land of flowing rivers, humid swamps, and lush savannas where wildlife was abundant.

The ancient rivers flowed east and west, possibly linking today's West African rivers such as the Niger and the Benue with the ancestors of the Nile in the east. And beneath the dry sands, water still flows through some of the valleys. Guided by *Columbia's* images, scientists discovered water in some of the Sahara's most arid places.

Other evidence confirms the Sahara's watery history. A 300-foot-high petrified coral reef courses across the landscape of southern Morocco. Near the oasis of Agadez in Niger a dinosaur graveyard has been discovered. Petrified tree trunks dot the deserts in Algeria and Egypt. Humans arrived in the Sahara much more recently—perhaps 10,000 years ago—as the waters were drying up. But the tools of Neolithic settlers litter the shores of the Selima's ancient rivers, and bone harpoons show that people once fished in the long-forgotten lakes of North Africa.

Even more recent evidence of a hospitable, temperate Sahara is found high on a sandstone plateau 5,000 feet above the now-dry plain of southern Algeria, in the heart of the Sahara. Here, at Tassili-n-Ajjer, hundreds of cave paintings, some 9,000 years old, depict men in loincloths herding long-horned cattle, women balancing baskets on their heads, and archers hunting antelopes and hippopotamuses.

The paintings trace the development and decline of the people, and the region's transformation into desert. The earliest pictures are of wild animals: buffalo, elephants, lions, and antelopes. Later, they show herdsmen with their domesticated animals. Paintings of two-wheeled war chariots, Nile boats, and camels tell of visits to Egypt far to the east. About 2,000 years ago, the painters left the area, which by then was rapidly becoming the desert of today.

And even in modern times, the Sahara continues to grow, creeping farther southward across Mali, Niger, Chad, and the Sudan at a rate of more than three miles a year. □

A radar image taken from the U.S. space shuttle *Columbia* in 1981 reveals a complex network of ancient river valleys now buried under the barren sands of the Sahara.

A LUMINOUS STAGE

E arth's atmosphere is a stage for a great range of luminous phenomena, as familiar as pearly dawns and as rare as the awesome tableaux of shining circles and arcs, spots and pillars that can surround the sun in geometric beauty and splash their astonishing symmetry from the horizon to the zenith. The candy-colored aurora borealis ripples in the polar sky, and lightning fills the air with split-second brilliance. Raindrops and ice crystals tease apart the spectral colors spun together in beams of light. Even on moonless nights, light never deserts the sky, for the atmosphere emits its own soft background glow.

Frictional Flashes

On rare occasions, storms generate shapes that glow like lightning, yet behave quite differently. During a heavy, wet March snow that surprised residents of the balmy Arizona desert city of Tucson in 1964, scattered flashes of light, apparently originating from the ground or close to it, brightened the snow every fifteen or twenty seconds. The flashes were less intense than lightning; moreover, no one heard any thunder, and local radios were free of the static that is usually associated with lightning bolts.

Another desert light display was witnessed in 1971 by a weather researcher in New Mexico's White Sands National Monument. As a thunderstorm swept through the area, the scientist was startled to see sparks some ten feet tall extending like bare, branchless, poles from the tops of several snow-white gypsum dunes.

Although such phenomena have not been studied extensively, the best scientific guess about both events is that the friction produced by wind-driven sand and snow sparks a release of the electrical charges such particles carry. □

The Glowing Andes

With a silent volley of bright flashes that subsides into a glow suffusing the sky, mountaintops sometimes discharge electricity into the atmosphere. Known as the Andes glow, this type of discharge is seen not only in the mountains of South America, but in the Alps and the Rockies as well. The glow is vast: It spreads high into the sky and across the mountain peaks and ridges for distances as great as three hundred miles.

The undulating rays of a discharge, which may include two dozen distinct flashes, are a brilliant yellow or orange, with an occasional streamer of green or pink light. As the glow develops, the distinct colors disappear and are replaced by pale yellow or white.

The Andes glow is especially spectacular if it is reinforced by an earthquake's repeated electrical discharges. During a great quake that struck Chile in 1906, observers reported that the whole sky seemed to be on fire. □

Saintly Fires

Vowing to circle the globe, Ferdinand Magellan set sail from Spain in September 1519. For the first few weeks, his ships plowed the well-traveled sea lane to the Cape Verde Islands, a colonial outpost 300 miles off Africa's Atlantic coast. But the islands were just the jumping-off place into the unknown, and on October 5, as the ships sailed south into uncharted waters, the crew grew uneasy about what lay ahead.

Uneasiness turned to fear when fierce storms struck, and the crew threatened to mutiny unless Magellan turned back. Suddenly, though, the tops of the masts came alive with globules of flickering, bluish light—in maritime lore, St. Elmo's fire, a supposed manifestation of the patron saint of mariners.

Sailor Antonio Pigafetta recorded in his journal of the voyage that "the holy body, that is to say St. Elmo, appeared to us many times in light . . . on an exceedingly dark night on the maintop where he stayed for about two hours or more to our consolation, for we were weeping. When that blessed light was about to leave us, . . . we called for mercy. And when we thought we were dead men, the sea suddenly grew calm."

What Magellan's men saw was a discharge of electrical voltage that had built up in the ships in response to low-lying, electrically charged clouds. Tall, pointed objects—masts, steeples, and flagpoles, for instance—provide the easiest conduit for electricity to pass into the air, where it excites gas molecules, causing them to glow softly.

The belief in the benevolence of

St. Elmo's fire is unfounded and dangerous, since the atmospheric conditions that produce it also increase the likelihood of lightning strikes at the very places where St. Elmo glows.

In fact, St. Elmo's fire was implicated in a catastrophe that radically changed air travel. On May 6, 1937, a large crowd turned out to watch the luxurious passenger airship *Hindenburg* land at Lakehurst, New Jersey, after a flight from Germany. The captain delayed the landing of the huge, hydrogen-filled craft for a time to allow a thunderstorm to pass. When the storm subsided to a drizzle, the airship began its descent, and crew members cast heavy landing ropes to the ground. To the crowd's horror, brilliant flames soon appeared around the tail of the *Hindenburg* and spread quickly to engulf it. Some of the people aboard were able to jump to safety, but thirty-six others perished.

Investigators concluded that leaking hydrogen, a highly combustible gas, had been ignited by an electrical current that surged upward from the ground along the *Hindenburg*'s landing ropes. The ordinarily harmless glow of St. Elmo's fire sparked a conflagration that destroyed the *Hindenburg* and the future of the airship as well. No dirigible ever carried a paying passenger again. □

The glow of St. Elmo's fire appears in a sailing ship's rigging, as portrayed in a nineteenth-century engraving.

Flashing Skies

The sequence of events that gives birth to lightning—whether the familiar flashes of a summer storm or the strange variations on that meteorological staple—remains something of a mystery. Even the perceived motion of lightning is an illusion, for the bolt that seems to descend from the sky in fact leaps up from the surface.

Lightning bolts between earth and sky are triggered when the negatively charged base of a cloud induces a positive charge in the ground. Streams of negative particles begin to probe downward, creating a conductive channel only an inch or two wide. When the channel reaches the ground—or, quite often, a tall building or tree—a powerful current zooms skyward. The brilliant flash occurs when the electrical charge excites the molecules of air in its path, causing them to release light.

Besides unleashing tremendous energy, lightning manifests a range of shapes and colors. Multiple-stroke flashes, in which several bolts travel the same channel at split-second intervals, are common. A brisk wind during a multiple flash can blow the conductive channel several feet sideways between flashes, producing "ribbon lightning"—parallel glowing lines *(right)*, each marking a different track of the conductive channel.

The rare bolt of bead lightning appears as a series of glowing pearls, dashes, or as a naval officer remarked of a flash he saw at sea, a disjointed spinal column. What force could snip lightning into pieces is as yet unknown, leading some scientists to suspect that the alternating segments and gaps— like the apparent downward course of lightning itself—are merely an optical illusion. □

Red, Rolling Thunder

The glowing red ball that Nancy Washington of Staffordshire, England, saw streaking toward her house during a storm in 1983 was definitely not an invention of her mind. It blasted a five-foot hole in the roof, then veered off to a nearby house, where it blew out the windows, popped electrical outlets from the walls, and left a hole in that roof as well.

More than a century before, a French tailor also had roof problems after a similar encounter. He had just finished dinner when a board covering his fireplace fell over and out popped a silent, fiery ball the size of a child's head. According to his account, the ball moved toward him like "a young cat that wants to rub itself against its master's legs." Next, it rose vertically for five feet or so, then moved toward a papered-over stovepipe hole above the mantle. The tailor claimed that the ball somehow removed the paper without burning it and proceeded to disappear up the chimney. A few moments later, a loud explosion destroyed the top of his chimney and hurled chunks of debris through several nearby roofs.

Both incidents were occurrences of what is called ball lightning. A typical ball ranges in size from six to twelve inches across. Its steady glow is most often red, orange, or yellow. Unlike the phenomenally fast bolt of stroke lightning, a ball moves at a relatively slow pace of just a few feet per second. Few balls survive for more than three seconds or so.

Because it is so short-lived and cannot be reproduced in the laboratory, ball lightning has eluded scientific explanation. Indeed, there are many scientists who consider it a figment of human imagination rather than a force of nature. Others, though, postulate that the lightning balls are a plasma, a superheated gas whose atoms have been stripped of their electrons. A plasma is considered a fourth state of matter—along with the liquid, solid, and gaseous states—because it behaves in such distinctive ways. ☐

This rare photograph of the meandering path of ball lightning was taken by a Japanese student during an afternoon storm that occurred near the city of Nagano on July 25, 1987.

Anatomy of a Rainbow

The beautiful rainbow born of a showery summer afternoon can seem almost palpable. But the arc is a silken weaving of light, a brilliant image that exists only in the eye of the beholder, with no more substance than a reflection in glass. No two people see the same rainbow: There are as many bows as there are observers. If a viewer walks toward a rainbow, it retreats at an identical pace. And, because it is a construction of light alone, the arc can appear suddenly and vanish just as quickly.

Although several earlier thinkers had come close, René Descartes, versatile genius of the 1600s, was the first to work out the precise optical geometry that creates the rainbow. The requirements are sunshine, rain, and an observer standing between the two, back to the sun. When sunlight streams past the observer and penetrates a raindrop, it is first refracted, or bent. Then, after crossing the drop to the far inner surface, the light is reflected back toward the viewer. As this reflected light emerges from the raindrop on the same side it entered, it is refracted again and tilted at an angle of forty-two degrees to its original path from the sun. This tilt gives the bow majestic dimensions: It can reach halfway to the zenith—the highest point overhead—and spread across nearly half the horizon in front of the viewer.

Besides being rerouted, the light has shed its whiteness for the proverbial rainbow array. A generation after Descartes, Isaac Newton discovered the origin of the colors —many wavelengths composing sunlight, each with its own characteristic angle of refraction. The topmost of the rainbow's concentric bands is red. The successive colors below it are orange, yellow, green, blue, indigo, and violet. The rainbow's colors are purest when the raindrops are moderately large; they blur and soften when the drops are either small or giant size.

Aristotle described the rainbow's true form about 2,300 years ago: It is a circle, whose center is aligned with the observer and the sun. But the full circle can be seen only rarely—in the mist from a waterfall or from an airplane or a mountaintop. The shadow of the earth itself blocks the sunlight from completing the circle for viewers on the surface. □

A moonlit nighttime shower can create a gray-white, nearly invisible moonbow that contains all of the same colors as a rainbow by day, rendered indistinguishable by the dim light.

As shown in this diagram, a rainbow is formed as falling raindrops reflect the sun's rays at a forty-two degree angle to their original path. Thus to a viewer standing at precisely the right spot between the sun and the rain *(center)*, the bow is visible forty-two degrees above its center. If the earth did not block a portion of the sun's rays, each rainbow would form a complete circle.

One-Color Bows

Most rainbows boast a wide range of colors, but an occasional arc has—or seems to have—only one color. Near sunset, for example, a multicolored rainbow sometimes turns to brightest red, reflecting and refracting only the sun's longest, last, red rays. The red rainbow *(right)* remains suspended above the eastern horizon for several minutes after sunset because the red rays of sunlight still illuminate raindrops high in the sky. □

A DOUBLE rainbow arches through a spring shower on the plains of Canada's Saskatchewan Province. The two bows are separated by a characteristic dark space that is known as Alexander's Dark Band.

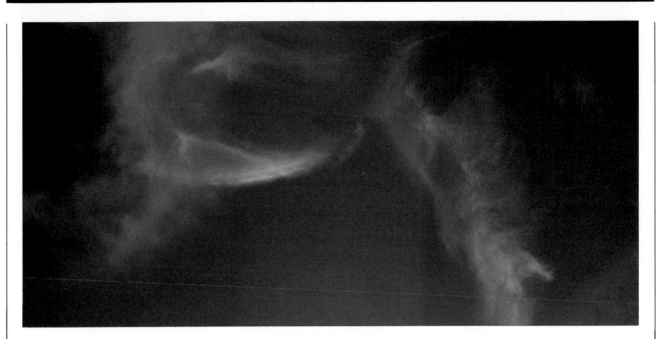

Visions in the Sun

On September 15, 1851, five baleful suns appeared to burn over Switzerland. Frightened peasants wondered if a disastrous conflagration was about to sweep the earth. The amazing sight was surpassed two decades later over Missouri, when the sun was joined by eight shining imitators.

The visions were examples of mock suns, sometimes called sundogs, formed by the refraction of light by ice crystals in the atmosphere. They normally appear as a pair of bright spots on either side of the sun, separated from it by about the width of an outstretched hand. But sundogs often coincide with rings around the sun called halos and related visual effects, compounding the dazzlement.

Some scientists have concluded that the mock suns and halo phenomena may have inspired historical and biblical accounts of visions. Meteorologist Freeman Hall has examined an account by the biblical prophet Ezekiel of two concentric wheels "so high that they were dreadful; and their rings were full of eyes round about them four." Above it all was a throne, glittering "like a sapphire." To Hall, the eyes may correspond to mock suns arranged on concentric halos, and the throne's seat may correspond to the beautifully colored circumzenithal arc, which

sometimes appears like an inverted rainbow high in the sky above a halo. Hall points out that thrones of Ezekiel's time often had concave, arc-shaped seats.

A powerful vision remarkably similar to a complex of halos and sundogs reportedly appeared to the Roman emperor Constantine. On the eve of battle in AD 312, the emperor saw an elaborate cross of light in the sky. Awed by the vision and believing it meant he had Christ's support, Constantine immediately converted from paganism to Christianity and triumphed in the ensuing battle.

What he could have seen, say scientists, is one of many possible combinations of halos, arcs, pillars, and mock suns. Whatever it was, the array of heavenly lights changed the course of history. With Constantine's conversion, Christianity was transformed from a despised sect to the religion of the Roman Empire. □

A Luminous Crown

On foggy nights, streetlamps are wreathed in coronas—hazy, luminous disks ringed by an orderly sequence of colors. The light waves from the lamps encounter countless small water droplets suspended in air; in a process called diffraction, these droplets separate the light waves into rings of their component colors.

The luminous wreaths are a diminutive version of the moon's corona—the only lunar phenomenon that is bright enough for its colors to be distinguished. Like a streetlamp's corona, the moon's is made by uniformly small droplets of water in the atmosphere. The smaller the drops, the larger the corona becomes, and the more uniform their size, the more intensely its colors gleam. Because lunar coronas betray the presence of moisture in the atmosphere, they are thought by some people to be harbingers of approaching storms. There is little evidence for such a belief, however.

Though rarely seen due to the sun's brilliance, solar coronas—particularly those called Bishop's rings, which are not caused by moisture—may also be bright and beautiful. Bishop's rings take their name from the Reverend Sereno E. Bishop of Hawaii, who recorded detailed observations of a spectacular solar corona in early September 1883. This ring was huge, and his sighting was confirmed by others, who reported giant solar coronas—and lunar ones—throughout the world. Their source was soon identified: Indonesia's Krakatau volcano, which had erupted with stupendous force on August 27, belching up fine dust that circled the globe *(pages 73-74)*. Since Bishop's discovery, the rings that bear his name have been noted in the aftermath of numerous volcanic eruptions. □

Divine Favor

Early one sparkling morning in the sixteenth century, the Italian artist Benvenuto Cellini was strolling with a friend through a dew-laden field. Facing away from the sun to avoid the glare, they were chatting amiably when Cellini spied a bright white halo ringing the shadow of his head. He saw no halo on his friend's shadow—a phenomenon that the never-humble Cellini pronounced as yet another sign of his own unique, divinely inspired gifts.

What the artist glimpsed in the dewy grass that morning would come to be known as Cellini's halo, but it is more commonly called by its German name, Heiligenschein, "light of the holy one." However, the phenomenon is a common one, hardly limited to the gifted or saintly.

The Heiligenschein *(above)* is produced by the reflection and refraction of sunlight by dewdrops at such an angle that each viewer's halo is his or her own, unseen by others. Cellini's companion on that sunny morning can thus be forgiven if he took exception to the artist's excited reaction to the sign. From where the companion stood, Cellini's shadow was unadorned, whereas his own seemed singled out for divine favor. □

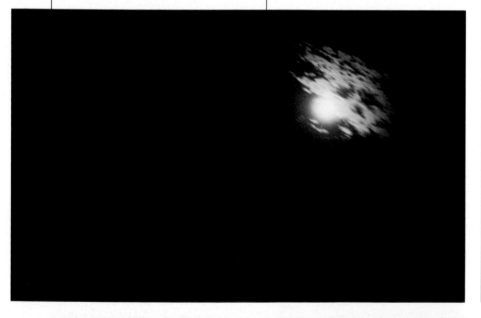

A prairie moon is encircled by a corona of light passing through thin clouds above the state of North Dakota.

Wreaths of Glory

From an airliner flying high above the clouds, a passenger watching the plane's shadow on the cloud below may see a glory—a particolored ring of light surrounding the shadow *(right)*.

The glory's origins are in the water droplets of the cloud, which reflect and bend light waves from the sun, separating them into their component colors of red, green, and blue. Like a rainbow, each glo-ry is the sole visual property of the person who sees it. And while glories are most frequently seen by air travelers (they are also known as pilot's bows) an occasional lucky ground-bound person—one standing on a mountaintop in the early morning, for example—may spot the shadow of his or her own head wreathed in glory against a cloud or a fogbank. Sometimes, the crown may have as many as five colored rings and a fogbow—a final faint, white ring. Regrettably, this glorious diadem remains invisible to all but its wearer. □

Monster in the Mountain Mist

Among the cloudy ridges of Germany's Harz Mountains, a creature of enormous proportions is said to lurk. Named the Brocken specter—after the range's highest peak, the Brocken—the legendary giant casts an enormous shadow on the mists that frequently wreathe the mountains. It is said that the specter sometimes wears a headdress of oak leaves and brandishes an uprooted pine tree.

Visual effects such as the Brocken specter can be seen throughout the world, wherever the sky and the terrain are such that the sun casts the shadow of the viewer—apparently much larger than life-size—on clouds or fog.

Psychologists speculate that witnesses are tricked into misjudging the vision's actual size because the projected shadow appears flat and thus lacks many of the three-dimensional cues that are normally used to judge size and distance. So, when trees and other objects appear together with a human shadow, the mind sees an apparition that seems to be as tall as a tree. Supposedly, the Brocken specter has frightened a number of climbers so badly that they have fallen to their deaths. □

Framed by a colorful Brocken bow, a Brocken specter is cast on clouds near Lake Lucerne in Switzerland.

A NOCTILUCENT CLOUD glows in the night sky fifty miles above Saskatchewan. Too tenuous to be seen by day, such high clouds become visible during subpolar summer twilights, when sunlight sparkles off the ice-covered dust—perhaps of extraterrestrial origin—that lies at the outer limits of the earth's atmosphere.

Shadowy Rays

At either end of the day, toward sunrise or sunset, when clouds building on the horizon obscure the sun but the sky overhead remains clear, dark bands sometimes arch across the heavens. Called crepuscular rays, they are the shadows cast by the cloud tops, separated by strips of sky lit by the sun. The shadows may also be cast by mountains or by unseen clouds below the horizon; then, the bands loom like ghostly fingers.

Sometimes, crepuscular rays arc from horizon to horizon, appearing far apart when they are directly overhead, then converging again opposite the sun. In fact, the rays are parallel throughout their course: The same trick of perspective that makes railroad tracks converge in the distance operates on the shadows. □

Shadows cast by the towering clouds, crepuscular rays fan across the Wisconsin sky at twilight.

A Sign of Light

On a clear night, far from city lights, the naked eye can detect a wedge of soft light that points toward the spot on the horizon where the sun set. Known as zodiacal light, it lies along the plane of the earth's orbit, called the ecliptic, and is named for the ecliptic's twelve subdivisions, the zodiac.

In the plane of the ecliptic is a vast cloud of debris left over from the formation of the planets. When sunlight hits the particles, which range from microscopic flecks of dust to rocky chunks three feet across, it is reflected like countless tiny moons.

The zodiacal light is most visible two hours after sunset at the spring equinox, when it travels a relatively short pathway through the atmosphere, whose gases and dust tend to scatter and reduce the glow. □

A Map in the Sky

The sky itself can provide polar travelers with the means to plot a safe course through ice-strewn waters and drifting ice floes. On days of mild overcast, bright and dark patches on the clouds' lower surface are, in effect, mirror images of the terrain below. These images result from the differing reflecting capacities of snow, ice, and water. When light strikes bright white snow or ice, for example, most of it is reflected upward to brighten the clouds. A dark surface such as open water reflects less light, and the clouds above it remain relatively dark.

The result is a so-called cloud map—bright sky signifying snow or ice below, dark sky betraying open water—which under ideal conditions can mirror points that lie thirty miles beyond the normal limits of vision.

Arctic sailors and ice travelers long ago adapted the phenomenon to their own special needs. Sailors stand watch against "ice blinks"— white patches on darker clouds that indicate sea ice and call for a change in course. On the other hand, a dark area ahead—known as a "water sky" because it betrays the presence of open water— means danger or at least a detour for the sojourner crossing an ice field on foot.

Anthropologist and explorer Vilhjalmur Stefansson, who traveled long distances over the sea ice of the north, reported that during a 1914 expedition the water sky showed cracks all about them. But "by keeping our eyes on the cloud map above we were able to travel sometimes a day at a time without even seeing water." □

Peering over the Edge

A millennium and more ago, mirages may have emboldened European sailors to set out across the uncharted North Atlantic. Choosing an illusory landmark to guide such a journey was not madness, but a clever exploitation of a phenomenon seen off far northern Europe's coasts. Known as the arctic mirage or, from the Icelandic, the *hillingar* effect, it is a so-called superior mirage that raises an image vertically and may have an extraordinarily lifelike look.

An arctic mirage develops when a very cold surface is covered by an air mass whose temperature increases steadily with altitude, causing light from an object to be bent in an arc whose curve matches that of the earth. Thus, the image can travel hundreds of miles and give the viewer an ability to "see" over the edge of the horizon. In 1939, for instance, a ship's captain claimed he saw Iceland's Snaefelljökull volcano from a distance of 300 miles.

According to some researchers who have studied the hillingar effect, there is tantalizing evidence in Celtic and Norse legends that the peoples of the North Atlantic may have learned from long experience that arctic mirages contain reliable information about what lies beyond the horizon. Around the year 800, Celts from the Faeroe Islands north of Scotland set out in their small, hide-covered coracles on the 200-mile journey to Iceland, and investigators speculate that they used a mirage to guide them. Similar phenomena may have guided Icelandic settlers under Erik the Red westward to Greenland in 980. And from there, other explorers may have used the images to arrive on the shores of North America. □

A Morning Mirage

As a man idly watches two boys on the other side of a shallow seaside inlet *(below)*, their morning stroll seems to turn into a miraculous event. One moment they are walking on the beach, and the next they are walking on the water. This startling sight is a mirage conjured up by the atmosphere. When temperature differences in adjoining air layers cause major changes in density, the atmosphere acts like a lens, bending light from its normally straight course. But the brain unconsciously assumes that the light of every image seen by the eye has traveled in a straight line—even when the image is distorted or misplaced. Thus can boys appear to walk on water.

On the morning of their walk, air that chilled during the night moved from the land out over the inlet. The warmer water heated the lowest layer of air, creating conditions ripe for the apparent feat— two layers of air differing in temperature and density. When the boys' image passed from the warmer (and so less dense), lower layer to the cooler and denser air above, it was shifted downward. To the man across the water, the horizon appeared to have sunk, carrying the beach and the boys' feet out of view to create the illusion that they were walking on the inlet. □

Although a mirage makes them appear to walk on Washington's Puget Sound, the boys are strolling on a sand spit.

The Fairy's Palace

Every now and again over the Strait of Messina, which divides Italy and Sicily, a construction of castles, balconied palaces, and crowded streets dances and shimmers between water and air.

Called the Fata Morgana, for the mythical Morgan le Fay—King Arthur's fairy half sister, who supposedly lived in a crystal palace beneath the sea—the tableau is a mirage. It is formed from the images of the rippling sea or, occasionally, a combination of the sea and actual distant buildings, cliffs, and trees gathered and distorted by layers of hot and cold air over the strait. Shifting winds further ripple the images, causing the Fata Morgana to oscillate between sea and sky, between brightness and darkness, between castles, columns, and forests.

Similar mirages, now also called Fata Morgana, have been sighted over large bodies of water and ice fields elsewhere in the world. The Silent City of Alaska appears every year on the Muir Glacier and is said by some extravagant observers to be a remarkable long-distance mirage of the city of Bristol, England, some 2,500 miles away. Its more prosaic origin is the jagged terrain of Alaska itself, visually transformed by layers of air. □

Early Spring Sunshine

In the fall of 1597, impassable arctic sea ice forced Dutch explorer Willem Barents and his crew to winter on the northern island of Novaya Zemlya, above Siberia. The long arctic night descended, and for weeks the sun stayed below the horizon. Then, one noon in late January, Barents was astonished to see the sun's rim peek over the southern horizon, two weeks ahead of its well-known schedule.

Barents had witnessed what has come to be called the Novaya Zemlya mirage, which develops when sunlight enters a layer of extremely cold air at the surface. This layer serves as a kind of duct, bending the light with the earth's curvature—sometimes far enough so that the sun itself appears to emerge from below the arctic horizon, bringing a premature image of spring. □

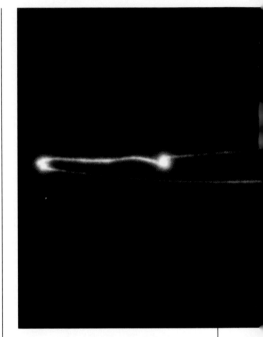

Twinkling

Every night, the stars perform their complex twinkling dance. Seen from the earth, they change in size, brighten and dim, and sometimes flash with a rainbow of colors. The delicate display is staged not by the stars themselves, but by the earth's atmosphere. Each time the density of the air changes in the line of sight between the heavens and earth, the stars scintillate. This happens continually, as weather and wind churn the air.

Air also acts as a prism, refracting, or bending, the component colors of starlight by varying degrees. Because refraction sets colors on slightly different paths, each is bent and rippled by the atmosphere independent of the others, creating shimmering, multicolored images of the stars. The brightest stars sparkle like a tray full of gemstones.

The stars look brighter on cold nights because the cold, dense air is more stable and uniform than warm, moist air, and starlight passes through with relatively little distortion. □

Atmospheric haze and motion cause the star cluster Pleiades to twinkle in the night sky.

West Texas Ghost Lights

Texas homesteader Robert Ellison must have felt a flash of fear when he saw what looked like campfires burning across a lonely plain. This was 1883, and the Apaches were not happy about settlers such as Ellison who were invading their territory. But as he watched, it became clear to Ellison that no Apaches lurked in the shadows. Unlike campfires, these lights floated and bounced amid the scrubby brush, almost playfully. Although Ellison no longer feared for his scalp, he remained justifiably anxious about just what was lighting up the night.

Ellison's discovery—the so-called Marfa lights, named after a town that sprang up nearby—is a classic instance of the ghost-light phenomenon. Appearing out of

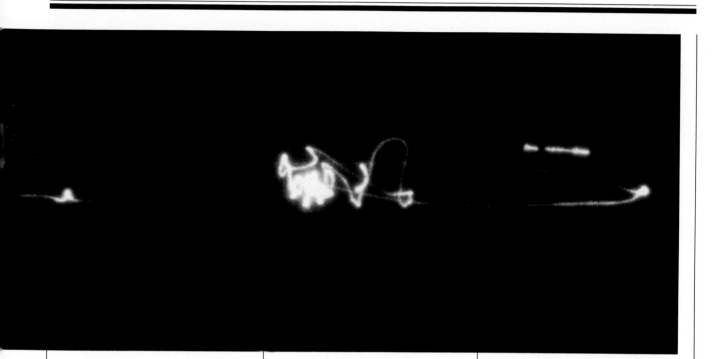

nowhere, a glowing mass bobs, darts, wiggles, and floats, rarely going higher than the treetops. The shape is usually spherical or oval, ranging up to three feet in diameter. A pale blue or white glow is most common, but sometimes it shifts to green or red.

Most ghost lights put in irregular appearances, but the Marfa lights are visible on most nights in every season. Many thousands of witnesses have watched them dancing in the dark over the past century. They are unquestionably real.

From the beginning, people were eager to explain the phenomenon, and Marfa storytellers and myth-makers let their imaginations go. The lights were said to be the spirits of buffaloes, penitential Indian warriors, a blind Indian princess seeking her lost lover, a vengeful sheriff perpetually pursuing his wife's murderer, or the body parts of a dismembered woodsman.

If no credence can be given to these fanciful tales, it is also true that no more rational cause has been pinpointed. Elsewhere, some ghost lights turn out to be will-o'-the-wisps—methane gas, emitted by decaying matter in a swampy area, that somehow ignites. But west Texas is arid, and Marfa is no exception. Superficially, the Marfa lights resemble the glowing balls of static electricity called St. Elmo's fire, but the conditions to create it do not exist there. Nor have geologists found phosphorescent minerals that might account for the glow.

According to some scientists, the most plausible hypothesis is a phenomenon called atmospheric tunneling—a kind of mirage in which light is refracted, so that it follows the contour of the earth over long distances. In an 1973 attempt to prove the tunneling theory, geologists Pat Kenney and

A time exposure captures the erratic movement of Texas's Marfa lights on an evening in September 1986. A car's headlights made the short straight line seen on the right.

Elwood Wright took bearings that would allow them to plot the lights' movements and relate them to the movements of automobile headlights from a distant highway. One night, however, they watched as one ghost light traced a loop and another moved back and forth "like a rocker on a rocking chair"—unlikely maneuvers for a car's headlights.

Other possible sources of refracted light at Marfa are planets and stars. Although they do not seem bright enough, these celestial bodies do have a historical advantage over headlights: They, like the Marfa lights, were visible well before the appearance of the automobile. □

Light Shows

More often than not, the aurora borealis is a shapeless pink glow or a whitish arch of light in the northern night sky. Half a world away, in the high latitudes of the southern hemisphere, the aurora australis puts on a similarly modest display. But when an extraordinary surge of electrically charged particles escapes from the sun—as happens periodically during sunspot cycles—the demure auroras erupt in magnificent spectacle several days later near the poles.

One such display was witnessed by a British writer, Roger Pilkington, over the Baltic Sea on a summer evening in 1962. He saw first a flicker, then a glow that reached halfway to the zenith. "This area grew brighter and redder, almost as though aflame, bands of purple light darting out from it to vanish in a flickering green," he wrote. "Slowly, . . . giant folds began to form and ripple like a gorgeously colored cloth of shot silk stirred by the wind. Rays like those of searchlights pierced the sky to the right, striking fanwise from the infinity of space." After an hour, the aurora faded.

The light of an aurora is emitted by oxygen and nitrogen atoms and

The shimmering curtain of the aurora borealis, or northern lights, brightens the night sky over Sudbury, Massachusetts, in 1982 (above). In the picture at right, taken from an altitude of 218 miles, an aurora appears as a ribbon of fire arcing across the earth's atmosphere. It was photographed in 1985 by Robert Overmeyer, pilot of the U.S. space shuttle *Challenger*.

molecules after they collide with the charged solar particles. The different colors appear at different altitudes. One hundred twenty miles or more above the earth's surface, red light dominates. Lower, the light turns green; in the lowest part of the aurora, some fifty or sixty miles above the earth, it is purplish.

The aurora is one of nature's freest spirits, taking on innumerable forms—some of which do not appear consistent with accepted scientific understanding. For example, one correspondent told the *Royal Astronomical Society of Canada Journal* about an especially brilliant aurora over Winnipeg that seemed to project thin streamers down until they touched the earth. But most scientists hold that auroras never approach closer than about fifty miles. □

The Green Sun

Occasionally, when the evening sun is about to disappear below a low, unobstructed horizon, the tiny bit of disk still visible turns brilliant green. Called the green flash because it lasts so briefly, the phenomenon is visible only when the atmosphere is so clear that it refracts, or bends, sunlight as neatly as a prism, separating it into its spectral colors.

The colored images of the sun are arrayed one above the other —purple at the top, red at bottom. However, violet and blue light waves are readily scattered by the atmosphere, and their images are rendered practically invisible. Nearest the ground, red light is bent only slightly, so it is the first color to be blocked by the earth as the sun slips below the horizon. At that instant, the dying light is virtually stripped of every color except one—green, which flashes briefly and unexpectedly before being overshadowed.

On a rare evening when the air is preternaturally clear and the scattering of light is minimal, the flash phenomenon can surpass itself, as green gives way instantaneously to blue, then purple, and finally, in the last second of light, a brilliant violet. □

Blue Skies and Flaming Sunsets

Earth's blue sky is an oddity, an exception to the near-universal blackness of space. Even at high noon on the moon, the sky looks like pitch; an astronaut peering skyward from the brightly lit lunar surface sees the stars ablaze across the firmament. Yet the earth's daytime sky is so bright that even the brightest stars are obscured by a curtain of blue.

What makes the difference is earth's atmosphere. It contains minute obstacles—molecules of gas, water droplets, and dust particles—that deflect some of the sun's light waves from their downward course and scatter them in all directions. As a result, light fills the sky. But not all light: Some components of the sun's rays—the shorter waves at the blue end of the spectrum—are scattered more than others, making blue the color that infuses the atmosphere of earth.

The longer waves of orange and red light are less affected by the atmospheric particles—moving like large ocean waves that flow over small rocks without breaking. At sunset, as the sun drops toward the horizon and light must make an ever-longer journey through the earth's atmosphere, it is the persistent, long red waves that reach the eye most abundantly, washing the evening world with red and orange. □

Two seemingly identical photos reveal a continuously blue sky. At left is a normal exposure taken at a farm near Milwaukee, Wisconsin, at noon; at right is a four-minute time exposure taken at 10:30 p.m., which reveals the same color sky by moonlight.

Gases from the eruption of Mexico's El Chicon volcano in 1982 produced this blood-red sunset over New Jersey.

Green Moons and Bright Afterglows

The deep purple glow that sometimes lingers in the sky after sunset has inspired generations of poets and songwriters. This magical luminosity owes its presence to a hazy sky that mixes the red rays of sunset with blue from above, producing purple light.

Dense clouds of volcanic particles can scatter the longer wavelengths of light to paint bizarrely gorgeous effects. After the colossal explosion of Indonesia's Krakatau in 1883 propelled a huge quantity of volcanic dust into the atmosphere *(pages 73-74)*, observers around the world reported such surreal sights as an emerald green crescent moon against a deep crimson sunset. Still more dramatic was a sort of second sunset that rekindled the west after darkness had fallen and the first stars had appeared. Apparently, a very high dust cloud scattered sunlight to create this brilliant afterglow, which one witness described as "a vast blood-red sheet." On some evenings, the afterglow lasted as long as an hour. □

ACKNOWLEDGMENTS

The editors wish to thank these individuals and institutions for their valuable assistance in the preparation of this volume:

Drucella Anderson, National Transportation Safety Board, Washington, D.C.; François Avril, Département des Manuscrits, Bibliothèque Nationale, Paris; Barry F. Beck, Florida Sinkhole Research Institute, University of Central Florida, Orlando; Hanno Beck, Geographisches Institut, Universität-Bonn, Bonn; Charles R. Bentley, University of Wisconsin, Madison; Carol S. Breed, U.S. Geological Survey, Flagstaff, Ariz.; Larry A. Chitwood, U.S. Forest Service, Bend, Ore.; James Clarke, U.S. Geological Survey, Reston, Va.; Michele Conte, Servizio Meteorologico, Meteorologico dell' Aeronautica Militare, Rome; Peter J. Crane, Mount Washington Observatory, Gorham, N.H.; Richard M. DeAngelis, National Oceanographic Data Center, Washington, D.C.; John S. Derr, Albuquerque Seismic Laboratory, N.Mex.; Dennis di Cicco, *Sky and Telescope*, Belmont, Mass.; Robert F. Dill, San Diego; Calif.; Giuditta Dolci-Favi, F.A.O., Rome; George E. Ericksen, U.S. Geological Survey, Reston, Va.; Eric Essene, Department of Geology, University of Michigan, Ann Arbor; Joan Frisch, National Center for Atmospheric Research, Boulder, Colo.; Robert Fudali, Smithsonian Department of Mineral Sciences, Smithsonian Institution, Washington, D.C.; James Gleason, Department of Mineral Sciences, Smithsonian Institution, Washington, D.C.; Joseph H. Golden, National Oceanic and Atmospheric Administration, Washington, D.C.; Bonnie Gordon, International Oceanographic Foundation, Sea Frontiers, Virginia Key, Fla.; Robert G. Greenler, Department of Physics, University of Wisconsin, Milwaukee; C. Vance Haynes, Jr., Department of Anthropology and Geosciences, University of Arizona, Tucson; Robert Hessler, Scripps Institution of Oceanography, University of California-San Diego, La Jolla; David H. Hickcox, Department of Geology and Geography, Ohio Wesleyan University, Delaware, Ohio; Klaus P. Hoinka, DFVLR, Oberpfaffenhofen, Wesseling, West Germany; Ross R. Hopkins, Death Valley National Monument, Death Valley, Calif.; Thomas Horne, Bethesda, Md.; Tom C. Hutchinson, Department of Botany, University of Toronto, Ontario; Sherwood B. Idso, U.S.D.A. Water Conservation Laboratory, Phoenix, Ariz.; Gerd Jendritzky, Deutscher Wetterdienst, Freiburg; Maureen Joubert, Embassy of South Africa, Washington, D.C.; William Laynor, Bureau of Technology, National Transportation Safety Board, Washington, D.C.; Roy S. Lewis, Enrico Fermi Institute and the Department of Chemistry, University of Chicago, Chicago; Patricia A. Lockridge, National Geophysical Data Center, Boulder, Colo.; Donald Loker, Niagara Falls Public Library, Niagara Falls; David K. Lynch, Topanga, Calif.; John F. McCauley, Northern Arizona University, Sedona; Michael Matson, NOAA/NESDIS, Washington, D.C.; G. T. Meaden, Tornado and Storm Research Organisation, Wiltshire, England; Terence Meaden, Bradford-on-Avon; Bruce Mehlhaff, Central Library, Rapid City; James R. Miller, South Dakota School of Mines and Technology, Rapid City; Kathy Miller, Oregon Fish and Wildlife, Bend, Ore.; Fabrizio Mori, Rome; Antonio Nazzaro, Naples: Thomas Parish, Department of Atmospheric Science, University of Wyoming, Laramie; Oregon Historical Society, Portland; Waverly Person, U.S. Geological Survey, Denver; Kenneth Rahn, University of Rhode Island, Narragansett; Kenneth L. Rancourt, Mount Washington Observatory, Gorham, N.H.; Robert J. M. Rickard, London; B. Ben Salem, F.A.O., Rome; Angela Schuh, Balneologisches Institut, Universität-Munich, Munich; Eugene Shoemaker, U.S. Geological Survey, Flagstaff, Ariz.; James Titus, Climate Change Division, EPA, Washington, D.C.; Ornello Valetti, Archivio Storico Comunale, Brescia, Italy; Alta S. Walker, U.S. Geological Survey, Reston, Va.; Steve Warren, Department of Atmospheric Sciences, University of Washington, Seattle; John A. Whitehead, Woods Hole Oceanographic Institution, Woods Hole, Mass.; Dewi Williams, British Information Services, New York; Richard S. Williams, Jr., U.S. Geological Survey, Reston, Va.

PICTURE CREDITS

The sources for the illustrations that appear in this book are listed below. Credits from left to right are separated by semicolons; from top to bottom by dashes.

Cover: Comstock, inset, J. Zuckerman/Westlight. **3:** J. Zuckerman/Westlight. **7:** H. D. Thoreau/Westlight, inset, Richard Woldendorp, Photo Index, Perth, Western Australia. **8:** United States Geological Survey (USGS). **9:** Syndication International Ltd., London. **10:** Artwork by Fred Holz. **11:** W. C. Mendenhall/USGS. **12-13:** Arnold Genthe, Library of Congress; San Jose Mercury News/Sygma. **14:** From *Messina e Reggio*, published by Libreria Bonanzinga, Messina, 1977, overlay photo, Brogi/Alinari, Florence. **15, 16:** NOAA, National Geophysical Data Center, Boulder, Colorado. **17:** From *The Complete Encyclopedia of Illustration*, by Johann G. Heck, Park Lane, New York, 1979. **18:** William M. Brown III/USGS. **19:** Darrell Herd/USGS. **20:** Courtesy Dorothy Silva. **21:** A. S. Navoy/USGS. **22:** George Plafker/USGS. **23:** From *Music: A Pictorial Archive of Woodcuts and Engravings*, selected by Jim Harter, Dover Publications, Inc., New York, 1980. **24:** © Kim Heacox/Earth Images—© Terry Domico/Earth Images. **25:** Jakob J. Møller, Tromsø Museum, Tromsø. **26:** Larry Sherer, courtesy Smithsonian Natural History Museum, Smithsonian Institution—The Photographic Library of Australia. **27:** Richard Woldendorp, Photo Index, Perth, Western Australia—Larry Sherer, courtesy Smithsonian Natural History Museum, Smithsonian Institution. **28:** David Cupp, © National Geographic Society, 1969. **29:** Larry Sherer, courtesy Smithsonian Natural History Museum, Smithsonian Institution. **30:** Western Australian Museum. **31:** L. Lee/Westlight, inset, © 1989 Warren Faidley/Weatherstock. **32-33:** Library of Congress; UPI/Bettmann Newsphotos. **34:** Gordon Baer/Black Star. **35:** The Bettmann Archive—artwork by Time-Life Books. **36-37:** NASA/Johnson Space Center, Houston (#511-35-075); artwork by Gene Garbowski. **38:** AP/Wide World Photos. **39:** Dr. Sherwood B. Idso—Fil Hunter. **40:** Bruce Brander/Photo Researchers. **41:** © 1989 Warren Faidley/Weatherstock. **42-43:** © 1989 Warren Faidley/Weatherstock; Steve Albers. **44:** Art Resource. **45:** Culver Pictures. **46-47:** George Gerster/Comstock (2)—Loren McIntyre. **48-49:** William Patrek; Dr. G. T. Meaden, Ceres/Torro, Bradford-on-Avon—B. Fuhrer, © A.N.T./N.H.P.A., Sussex. **51:** C. Aurness/Westlight, inset, R. J. M. Rickard/Bedford County Press. **52:** Courtesy of Science Service. **53:** Field Museum of Natural History, Chicago (#79617)—UPI/Bettmann Newsphotos. **54-55:** National Autonomous University of Mexico, Institute of Geology. **56:** Photo A.J.R., courtesy Department Library Services, American Museum of Natural History (#284965)—James M. Baker, Omaha. **57:** Technology Application Center, University of New Mexico. **58-59:** From *The Complete Encyclopedia of Illustration*, by Johann G. Heck, Park Lane, New York, 1979; Oregon Historical Society (#OrHi 56119). **60:** Charles and Nancy Knight, National Center of Atmospheric Research/National Science Foundation. **61, 62:**

National Center of Atmospheric Research/ National Science Foundation. **63:** *The Cincinnati Enquirer*—The Mansell Collection, London. **64:** Paul N. Gross, Warrington, Cheshire. **65:** From *Animals: 1419 Copyright-Free Illustrations of Mammals, Birds, Fish, Insects*, selected by Jim Harter, Dover Publications, Inc., New York, 1979—R. J. M. Rickard/Bedford County Press. **66:** Fortean Picture Library, Wales—*The Queensland Times*, Brisbane, Australia. **67:** From *Animals: 1419 Copyright-Free Illustrations of Mammals, Birds, Fish, Insects*, selected by Jim Harter, Dover Publications, Inc., New York, 1979—Covello & Covello Photography. **68:** Reproduced by permission of the Western Mail and Echo Ltd., Cardiff, Wales. **69:** M. Angelo/Westlight, inset, A. E. Harnoiot. **70:** Gianni Dagli Orti, Paris. **71:** Giuseppe Leone, Ragusa, from *De Aetna*, Sellerio Editore, Palermo. **72:** USGS. **73:** Krakatau 1883, by Tom Simkin and Richard S. Fiske, Smithsonian Institution, 1983. **74:** © 1989 Dorian Weisel/Volcanic Resources. **75:** Library of Congress (LC-USZ62:25077). **76:** USGS—A. E. Harnoiot. **77:** Sigurgeir Jónasson. **78:** © 1989 Warren Faidley/ Weatherstock. **79:** Mary Evans Picture Library, London. **80:** © 1989 Warren Faidley/ Weatherstock. **81:** *Weatherwise* magazine; Hall of History, General Electric Company. **82-83:** Tom Hutchinson and Magda Havas, Institute for Environmental Studies, University of Toronto. **85:** M. Angelo/Westlight, inset, courtesy Greg Gordon, the Mount Washington Observatory. **86:** E. T. Archive, London. **88-89:** E. Valli/ A.N.A., Paris; Stuart Hurlbert. **90:** AP/Wide World Photos; The Bettmann Archive. **91:** UPI/ Bettmann Newsphotos. **92:** Courtesy Greg Gordon, the Mount Washington Observatory. **93:** Scala, Florence. **94:** Eliot Porter. **95:** M. A. McWhinnie for the National Science Foundation—Dale Brown. **96:** Dr. Mort D. Turner—Eliot Porter. **97:** © 1988 Sharon Chester. **98:** Library of Congress. **99:** B. Ross/Westlight, inset, Kazuyoshi Nomachi/Pacific Press Service. **100:** Dale Brown—Penny Rennicks. **101:** Artwork by Fred Holz. **102:** Rear Admiral Billings, U.S. Navy, NOAA/National Geophysical Data Center. **103:** Mark Sosin/Black Star—NOAA/ National Geophysical Data Center. **104:** H. Jesse Walker, Department of Geography and Anthropology, Louisiana State University. **105:** Paul R. Carlson and Robert Hall/USGS—Dudley Foster, Woods Hole Oceanographic Institution—Dr. Robert R. Hessler, Scripps Institute of Oceanography. **106-107:** Kazuyoshi Nomachi/ Pacific Press; Hiroju Kubota/Magnum. **108:** Culver Pictures, Inc. **109:** Eric Bouvet/Gamma Liaison. **110:** © C. C. Lockwood/Bruce Coleman. **111:** © Will McIntyre/Photo Researchers. **112:** Austin History Center, Austin Public Library. **113:** Loren McIntyre; Rosalie LaRue Faubia/ Bruce Coleman. **114:** USGS. **115:** Kul Bhatia, inset, Dennis di Cicco. **117:** Mary Evans Picture Library, London. **118:** © 1989 Warren Faidley/ Weatherstock. **119:** Courtesy Professor Yoshi-Hiko Ohtsuki, Waseda University, Tokyo. **120-121:** Artwork by Fred Holz. **122:** Robert Greenler—Gustavo Pocobelli. **123:** Tim Pickering—© 1983 Thomas Ives. **124:** Courtesy S. Bartsch-Winkler/USGS—Fred Schaaf. **125:** Robert Greenler—Dennis di Cicco. **126:** Steve Albers—Robert Greenler. **127:** Steve Albers. **128:** Alistair B. Fraser. **129:** Robert Greenler. **130-131:** The Royal Observatory, Edinburgh and Anglo-Australian Telescope Board; © 1986 James Crocker. **132-133:** Dennis di Cicco; NASA Johnson Space Center (#51D-116-005). **134:** Robert Greenler. **135:** Fred Schaaf.

BIBLIOGRAPHY

Books

ABC's of Nature. Pleasantville, N.Y.: Reader's Digest Association, 1984.

Academic American Encyclopedia. Princeton, N.J.: Aretê Publishing, 1980.

Ahrens, C. Donald. *Meteorology Today: An Introduction to Weather, Climate, and the Environment* (2d ed.). St. Paul: West Publishing, 1985.

Andrews, William. *Famous Frosts and Frost Fairs in Great Britain.* London: George Redway, 1887.

Antarctica. Sydney: Reader's Digest Services, 1985.

Baeyer, Ilans C. von. *Rainbows, Snowflakes, and Quarks: Physics and the World around Us.* New York: McGraw-Hill, 1984.

Bascom, Willard. *Waves and Beaches.* Garden City, N.Y.: Anchor Press/Doubleday, 1980.

Blair, Thomas A., and Robert C. Fite. *Weather Elements: A Text in Elementary Meteorology* (5th ed.). Englewood Cliffs, N.J.: Prentice-Hall, 1965.

Blumenstock, David I. *The Ocean of Air.* New Brunswick, N.J.: Rutgers University Press, 1959.

Boyer, Carl B. *The Rainbow: From Myth to Mathematics.* Princeton, N.J.: Princeton University Press, 1987.

Brueske, Judith M. *The Marfa Lights.* Alpine, Tex.: Ocotillo Enterprises, 1988.

Bullard, Fred M. *Volcanoes of the Earth* (2d ed.). Austin: University of Texas Press, 1984.

Cade, C. Maxwell, and Delphine Davis. *The Taming of the Thunderbolts.* London: Abelard-Schuman, 1969.

Calder, Nigel. *The Weather Machine.* New York: Viking Press, 1974.

Caldwell, John. *Desperate Voyage.* Leicester, U.K.: Ulverscroft, 1950.

Chapman, Sydney. *IGY: Year of Discovery: The Story of the International Geophysical Year.* Ann Arbor: University of Michigan Press, 1968.

Charton, Barbara. *The Facts On File Dictionary of Marine Science.* New York: Facts On File Publications, 1988.

Corbett, Edmund (Ed.). *Great True Stories of Tragedy and Disaster.* New York: Archer House, 1963.

Corliss, William R. (Comp.):

Anomalies in Geology: Physical, Chemical, Biological. Glen Arm, Md.: Sourcebook Project, 1989.

Carolina Bays, Mima Mounds, Submarine Canyons and Other Topographical Phenomena. Glen Arm, Md.: Sourcebook Project, 1988.

Earthquakes, Tides, Unidentified Sounds and Related Phenomena. Glen Arm, Md.: Sourcebook Project, 1983.

Handbook of Unusual Natural Phenomena. Garden City, N.Y.: Anchor Press/Doubleday, 1983.

Lightning, Auroras, Nocturnal Lights, and Related Luminous Phenomena. Glen Arm, Md.: Sourcebook Project, 1982.

Rare Halos, Mirages, Anomalous Rainbows and Related Electromagnetic Phenomena. Glen Arm, Md.: Sourcebook Project, 1984.

Tornados, Dark Days, Anomalous Precipitation, and Related Weather Phenomena. Glen Arm, Md.: Sourcebook Project, 1983.

Unknown Earth: A Handbook of Geological Enigmas. Glen Arm, Md.: Sourcebook Project, 1980.

Cornell, James C., Jr. *Nature at Its Strangest.* New York: Sterling, 1974.

Davison, Charles. *Great Earthquakes.* London: Thomas Murby, 1936.

Devereux, Paul, et al. *Earth Lights Revelation.* London: Blandford Press, 1989.

Encyclopædia Britannica (Vols. 10, 14, 23). Chicago: William Benton, 1960.

The Encyclopedia Americana: International Edition (Vol. 18). Danbury, Conn.: Grolier, 1983.

Erickson, Jon:
  The Mysterious Oceans. Blue Ridge Summit, Pa.: Tab Books, 1988.
  Violent Storms. Blue Ridge Summit, Pa.: Tab Books, 1988.

Facts & Fallacies. Pleasantville, N.Y.: Reader's Digest Association, 1988.

The Fascinating Secrets of Oceans & Islands. London: Reader's Digest Association, 1972.

Ferrara, Grace (Ed.). *The Disaster File: The 1970s.* New York: Facts On File, 1979.

Flatow, Ira. *Rainbows, Curve Balls and Other Wonders of the Natural World Explained.* New York: William Morrow, 1988.

Frazier, Kendrick. *The Violent Face of Nature.* New York: William Morrow, 1979.

Fujita, T. Theodore. *The Downburst: Microburst and Macroburst.* Chicago: Department of Geophysical Sciences, University of Chicago, 1985.

Gallant, Roy A. *Earth's Changing Climate.* New York: Four Winds Press, 1979.

Gates, David M. *Man and His Environment: Climate.* New York: Harper & Row, 1972.

Great Disasters. Pleasantville, N.Y.: Reader's Digest Association, 1989.

Greenler, Robert. *Rainbows, Halos, and Glories.* Cambridge: Cambridge University Press, 1980.

Groves, Don. *The Oceans: A Book of Questions and Answers.* New York: John Wiley & Sons, 1989.

Groves, Donald G., and Lee M. Hunt. *Ocean World Encyclopedia.* New York: McGraw-Hill, 1980.

Guinness Book of World Records 1989. New York: Sterling, 1988.

Hafnor, John. *Black Hills Believables.* Billings and Helena, Mont.: Falcon Press, 1983.

Hall, Freeman F., Jr. "Ezekiel's Wheels As a Complex Halo Phenomenon." *Topical Meeting on Meteorological Optics.* Incline Village, Nev.: Optical Society of America, 1983.

Hardy, Ralph, et al. *The Weather Book.* Boston: Little, Brown, 1982.

Heuer, Kenneth. *Rainbows, Halos, and Other Wonders: Light and Color in the Atmosphere.* New York: Dodd, Mead, 1978.

Hildreth, Wes. *Death Valley Geology: Rocks and Faults, Fans and Salts.* Death Valley, Calif.: Death Valley Natural History Association, 1976.

Hsü, Kenneth J. *The Mediterranean Was a Desert.* Princeton, N.J.: Princeton University Press, 1983.

Kals, W. S. *Your Health, Your Moods, and the Weather.* Garden City, N.Y.: Doubleday, 1982.

Kendig, Frank, and Richard Hutton. *Life-Spans: Or How Long Things Last.* New York: Holt, Rinehart & Winston, 1979.

Kendrick, T. D. *The Lisbon Earthquake.* London: Methuen, 1956.

King, H. G. R. *The Antarctic.* New York: Arco, 1969.

Kingston, Jeremy, and David Lambert. *Catastrophe and Crisis.* New York: Facts On File, 1979.

Kirk, Ruth. *Desert: The American Southwest.* Boston: Houghton Mifflin, 1973.

Können, G. P. *Polarized Light in Nature.* Translated by G. A. Beerling. Cambridge: Cambridge University Press, 1985.

Lane, Ferdinand C. *Earth's Grandest Rivers.* Garden City, N.Y.: Doubleday, 1949.

Lane, Frank W:
  The Elements Rage. Philadelphia: Chilton Books, 1965.
  The Violent Earth. Topsfield, Mass.: Salem House, 1986.

Larson, Peggy, and Lane Larson. *The Deserts of the Southwest.* San Francisco: Sierra Club Books, 1977.

LeMaire, T. R. *Stones from the Stars: The Unsolved Mysteries of Meteorites.* Englewood Cliffs, N.J.: Prentice-Hall, 1980.

Lewis, Richard S. *A Continent for Science: The Antarctic Adventure.* New York: Viking Press, 1965.

Limburg, Peter R., and James B. Sweeney. *102 Questions and Answers about the Sea.* New York: Julian Messner, 1975.

Lockhart, Gary. *The Weather Companion.* New York: John Wiley & Sons, 1988.

Longwell, Chester R., Richard Foster Flint, and John E. Sanders. *Physical Geology.* New York: John Wiley & Sons, 1969.

Louw, Gideon, and Mary Seely. *Ecology of Desert Organisms.* London: Longman, 1982.

Ludlum, David, and the Editors of Blair & Ketchum's Country Journal. *New England Weather Book.* Boston: Houghton Mifflin, 1976.

Ludlum, David M.:
  The American Weather Book. Boston: Houghton Mifflin, 1982.
  Early American Tornadoes, 1586-1870. Boston: American Meteorological Society, 1970.
  The Weather Factor. Boston: Houghton Mifflin, 1984.

Lynch, David K. *Atmospheric Phenomena.* San Francisco: W. H. Freeman, 1980.

McAlester, A. Lee. *The Earth: An Introduction to the Geological and Geophysical Sciences.* Englewood Cliffs, N.J.: Prentice-Hall, 1973.

McNamara, Ken. *Tektites.* Perth: Western Australian Museum, 1985.

McPhee, John. *The Control of Nature.* New York: Farrar Straus Giroux, 1989.

McSween, Harry Y., Jr. *Meteorites and Their Parent Planets.* Cambridge: Cambridge University Press, 1987.

Mather, Kirtley F. *The Earth beneath Us.* New York: Random House, 1964.

May, John. *Antarctica: A New View of the Seventh Continent.* New York: Doubleday, 1989.

Meaden, George Terence. *The Circles Effect and Its Mysteries.* Bradford-on-Avon, U.K.: Artetech Publishing, 1989.

Meinel, Aden, and Marjorie Meinel. *Sunsets, Twilights, and Evening Skies.* Cambridge: Cambridge University Press, 1983.

Michell, John, and Robert J. M. Rickard. *Phenomena: A Book of Wonders.* London: Thames & Hudson, 1977.

Miles, Elton. *Tales of the Big Bend.* College Station: Texas A&M University Press, 1976.

Miller, James R., Jr. *Rapid City Climate.* Rapid City: South Dakota School of Mines and Technology Foundation, 1986.

Mitchell, Richard Scott. *Dictionary of Rocks.* New York: Van Nostrand Reinhold, 1985.

Myles, Douglas. *The Great Waves.* New York: McGraw-Hill, 1985.

Mysteries of the Unexplained. Pleasantville, N.Y.: Reader's Digest Association, 1982.

Nash, Robert. *Darkest Hours.* Chicago: Nelson-Hall, 1976.

The New Encyclopædia Britannica (Vol. 7). Chicago: Encyclopædia Britannica, 1984.

New Illustrated Columbia Encyclopedia (Vols. 3, 9, 15, 16, 24). New York: Columbia University Press, 1979.

Our Awesome Earth: Its Mysteries and Its Splendors. Washington, D.C.: National Geographic Society, 1986.

Palmer, Robert. *The Blue Holes of the Bahamas.* London: Jonathan Cape, 1985.

Penick, James, Jr. *The New Madrid Earthquakes of 1811-1812.* Columbia: University of Missouri Press, 1976.

Preston, Richard. *The Search for the Edge of the Universe.* New York: Atlantic Monthly Press, 1987.

Putnam, William C. *Geology.* New York: Oxford University Press, 1964.

Rankin, William H. *The Man Who Rode the Thunder.* Englewood Cliffs, N.J.: Prentice-Hall, 1960.

Riley, Denis, and Lewis Spolton. *World Weather and Climate.* Cambridge: Cambridge University Press, 1974.

Ritchie, David. *The Ring of Fire.* New York: Atheneum, 1981.

Rosen, Stephen. *Weathering: How the Atmosphere Conditions Your Body, Your Mind, Your Moods—and Your Health.* New York: M. Evans, 1979.

Ruffner, James A., and Frank E. Bair. *The Weather Almanac.* Detroit: Gale Research, 1977.

Sandborn, William B. *Oddities of the Mineral World.* New York: Van Nostrand Reinhold, 1976.

Savage, Henry, Jr. *The Mysterious Carolina Bays.* Columbia: University of South Carolina Press, 1982.

Schaaf, Fred. *Wonders of the Sky.* New York: Dover Publications, 1983.

Schultz, Gwen. *Ice Age Lost.* Garden City, N.Y.: Anchor Press/Doubleday, 1974.

Shepard, Jean, and Daniel Shepard. *Earth Watch: Notes on a Restless Planet.* Garden City, N.Y.: Doubleday, 1973.

Smith, Howard E., Jr. *Killer Weather: Stories of Great Disasters.* New York: Dodd, Mead, 1982.

Stacy, Dennis. *The Marfa Lights: A Viewer's Guide.* San Antonio, Tex.: Seale & Stacy, 1989.

Strange Stories, Amazing Facts. Pleasantville, N.Y.: Reader's Digest Association, 1976.

Sutton, Ann, and Myron Sutton. *The Life of the Desert.* New York: McGraw-Hill, 1966.

Taber, Robert W., and Harold W. Dubach. *1001 Questions Answered about the Oceans and Oceanography.* New York: Dodd, Mead, 1972.

Thorndike, Joseph J., Jr. (Ed.). *Mysteries of the Deep.* New York: American Heritage, 1980.

Trefil, James S. *The Unexpected Vista: A Physicist's View of Nature.* New York: Charles Scribner's Sons, 1983.

Tributsch, Helmut. *When the Snakes Awake: Animals and Earthquake Prediction.* Translated by Paul Langner. Cambridge, Mass.: MIT Press, 1983.

Tufty, Barbara:
1001 Questions Answered about Earthquakes, Avalanches, Floods and Other Natural Disasters. New York: Dover Publications, 1969.
1001 Questions Answered about Storms and Other Natural Air Disasters. New York: Dodd, Mead, 1970.

Uman, Martin A.:
The Lightning Discharge. Orlando, Fla.: Academic Press, 1987.
Understanding Lightning. Carnegie, Pa.: Bek Technical Publications, 1971.

Viemeister, Peter E. *The Lightning Book.* Garden City, N.Y.: Doubleday, 1961.

Vitaliano, Dorothy B. *Legends of the Earth: Their Geologic Origins.* Bloomington: Indiana University Press, 1973.

The Weather Book. Boston: Little, Brown, 1982.

Weiner, Jonathan. *Planet Earth.* Toronto: Bantam Books, 1986.

Wells, Robert W. *Fire at Peshtigo.* Englewood Cliffs, N.J.: Prentice-Hall, 1968.

Weyman, Darrell, and Valerie Weyman. *Landscape Processes: An Introduction to Geomorphology.* London: George Allen & Unwin, 1977.

Wilcoxson, Kent H. *Chains of Fire: The Story of Volcanoes.* Philadelphia: Chilton Book Co., 1966.

Wood, Robert Muir. *Earthquakes and Volcanoes.* London: Mitchell Beazley, 1986.

The World Book Encyclopedia of Science: The Planet Earth (rev. ed.). Chicago: World Book, 1987.

Young, Louise B. *Earth's Aura.* New York: Alfred A. Knopf, 1977.

Young, Robert A. "The Airglow." In *Light from the Sky.* San Francisco: W. H. Freeman, 1980.

Periodicals

"Africa's River of Legend." *National Geographic,* May 1985.

Amos, Anthony F. "Green Iceberg Sampled in the Weddell Sea." *Antarctic Journal,* October 1978.

Anderson, Harry. "A Deadly Wall of Water." *Newsweek,* June 10, 1985.

"Archbald's Pot Hole World's Largest, Attracts Geologists." *Scranton Gazette,* July 8, 1970.

"The Aurora at Low Levels." *Royal Astronomical Society of Canada Journal,* 1934, Vol. 28, p. 335.

Baines, John. "Time and the River: The Nile and Ancient Egypt." *Unesco Courier,* September 1988.

Bajkov, A. D. "Do Fish Fall from the Sky?" *Science,* April 22, 1949.

Barton, John. "A True Fish Story." *Ann Arbor News,* July 24, 1986.

Benjamin, George J. "Diving into the Blue Holes of the Bahamas." *National Geographic,* September 1970.

"Black and White Icebergs." *Marine Observer,* January 1972.

Bloch, R., H. Z. Littman, and B. Elazari-Volcani. "Occasional Whiteness of the Dead Sea." *Nature,* September 23, 1944.

Bowen, Ezra. "Speaking of Snow Jobs." *Smithsonian,* March 1988.

Bower, Bruce. "The 'Killer Lake' of Cameroon." *Science News,* December 7, 1985.

Brennan, Michael. "Chunk of Winter Park Falls with House, Cars, City Pool." *Orlando Sentinel Star,* May 10, 1981.

Brinkmann, W. A. R. "What is a Foehn?" *Weather,* June 1971.

Brown, Joseph. "Rogue Waves." *Discover,* April 1989.

Brydon, H. Boyd. "Within the Aurora." *Royal Astronomical Society of Canada Journal,* 1935, Vol. 29, p. 118.

"Building Damaged by Hail." *Los Angeles Times,* May 24, 1972.

Caldwell, J. "On Sailing through a Waterspout." *Journal of Meteorology,* September 1986.

Cameron, T. Wilson. "Treachery of Freak Waves." *Marine Observer,* 1935, Vol. 55, p. 202.

Carey, John. "The Mystery of Arctic Haze." *Weatherwise,* April 1988.

Carlson, Paul R., and Herman A. Karl. "Development of Large Submarine Canyons in the Bering Sea, Indicated by Morphologic, Seismic, and Sedimentologic Characteristics." *Geological Society of America Bulletin,* October 1988.

Clarke, R. H. "The Morning Glory." *Weatherwise,* June 1983.

Clarke, R. H., R. K. Smith, and D. G. Reid. "The Morning Glory of the Gulf of Carpentaria: An Atmospheric Undular Bore." *Monthly Weather Review,* August 1981.

"Cold Wave in Hills Broken—Chinooks Run Mercury Ragged in Rapid City." *Rapid City Daily Journal,* January 22, 1943.

Colton, F. Barrows. "The Geography of a Hurricane." *National Geographic,* April 1939.

"Continued Cold Weather Forecast after Friday's Freakish Warmth." *Rapid City Daily Journal,* January 23, 1943.

Cook, Orange. "Ribbon Lightning." *Popular Science Monthly,* 1900, Vol. 56, p. 587.

Curtin, Barbara. "Garden in Sisters Runneth Over." *The Oregonian,* September 11, 1979.

"The Deadliest Tornado in American History." *Literary Digest,* April 4, 1925.

Donnelly, Sally B. "Around and Around in Circles." *Time,* September 18, 1989.

Dybwik, Dagfinn, and Jakob J. Møller. "Phenomenon in an Andøya Moor." *Ottar* (publication of the Tromsø Museum), 1988, no. 5, p. 15.

Ericksen, George E. "The Chilean Nitrate Deposits." *American Scientist,* July-August 1983.

"Europe's Bad Winter Is Cruel to the End." *Life,* March 12, 1956.

Everling, Anna. "Waterspouts." *Weatherwise,* July-August 1987.

"Family Cat Eats Well As Sardines Fall from the Sky." *Queensland Times,* February 7, 1989.

"Finders of Green Snow Report Itch." *Sacramento Bee,* April 10, 1953.

Fraser, Alistair B., and William H. Mach. "Mirages." *Scientific American,* January 1976.

"Freak Wave: South African Waters." *Marine Observer,* April 1982.

Fujiwhara, S. "The Horizontal Rainbow." *Monthly Weather Review,* July 1914.

Garner, Kenneth B. "Concretions Near Mt. Signal, Lower California." *American Journal of Science,* April 1936.

"Geothermal Energy." *Earth Science,* Summer 1986.

Gibbons, John F., II, and Steven Schlossman. "Rock Music." *Natural History*, December 1970.

"Gigantic Snowflakes." *Monthly Weather Review*, February 1915.

Glass, B. P. "Tektites." *Journal of Non-Crystalline Solids*, 1984, Vol. 67, pp. 333-344.

Glaze, Dean. "Kopperl's Close Encounter with Satan's Storm." *Meridian Tribune*, May 12, 1983.

Gordon, Greg:
"The Home of Boreas: Mount Washington's Meteorological Phenomena." *Mount Washington Observatory News Bulletin*, June 1980.
"Whadda You Guys Do Up There, Anyway?" *Mount Washington Observatory News Bulletin*, Spring 1984.

Grigoroff, Louis. "Falls Ran 'Dry' 111 Years Ago." *Niagara Falls Evening Review*, March 28, 1959.

"Hailstorm on the St. Lawrence." *Monthly Weather Review*, November 1901.

Hall, Roy S. "Inside a Texas Tornado." *Weatherwise*, April 1987.

Hamilton, Robert M. "Quakes along the Mississippi." *Natural History*, August 1980.

Havas, Magda, and Thomas C. Hutchinson. "The Smoking Hills: Natural Acidification of an Aquatic Ecosystem." *Nature*, January 1983.

Haynes, C. Vance, Jr. "Great Sand Sea and Selima Sand Sheet, Eastern Sahara: Geochronology of Desertification." *Science*, August 1982.

Haynes, C. Vance, Jr., et al. "Evidence for the First Nuclear-Age Recharge of Shallow Groundwater, Arba'in Desert, Egypt." *National Geographic Research*, 1987, Vol. 3, p. 431.

Hessler, Robert, Peter Lonsdale, and James Hawkins. "Patterns on the Ocean Floor." *New Scientist*, March 24, 1988.

Hickcox, David H. "How Hot Can It Get?" *Weatherwise*, June 1988.

Hinder, F. S. "Tadpoles." *English Mechanic*, 1911, Vol. 94, p. 62.

Hodgdon, Russell (Casey). "The Story of Lizzie Bourne." *Mount Washington Observatory News Bulletin*, September 1965.

Hodges, Kip. "Itacolumite: The Flexible Rock." *Rocks and Minerals*, June 1972.

Holzer, T. L., T. L. Youd, and T. C. Hanks. "Dynamics of Liquefaction during the 1987 Superstition Hills, California, Earthquake." *Science*, April 1989.

Horne, Thomas A. "The Deadly Wind." *AOPA Pilot*, August 1986.

Hoyt, Chuck. "Glacier Crumbles, Boat Hit by Gigantic Wave." *Anchorage Daily News*, July 10, 1958.

Hughes, Patrick. "The Year without a Summer." *Weatherwise*, June 1979.

Hurlbert, Stuart H., and Cecily C. Y. Chang. "Ancient Ice Islands in Salt Lakes of the Central Andes." *Science*, April 20, 1984.

"Ice Islands in the Andes." *New Scientist*, November 4, 1982.

"If a Tree Falls and No One Hears . . ." *Science News*, November 21, 1981.

Ilsü, Kenneth J. "When the Mediterranean Dried Up." *Scientific American*, December 1972.

Iyer, Pice. "Trail of Tears and Anguish." *Time*, June 10, 1985.

Kerr, Richard A. "Quake Prediction by Animals Gaining Respect." *Science*, May 16, 1980.

Kling, George W. "Seasonal Mixing and Catastrophic Degassing in Tropical Lakes, Cameroon, West Africa." *Science*, August 28, 1987.

Kol, Erzsebet. "The Snow and Ice Algae of Alaska." *Smithsonian Miscellaneous Collections*, 1942, Vol. 101, no. 16.

"Lake Baikal." *Unesco Courier*, October 1987.

"The Lake of Death." *Time*, September 8, 1986.

LeBlanc, Jerry. "Tales of the Wild Ocean." *Oceans*, August 1986.

Lessard, Arthur G. "The Santa Ana Wind of Southern California." *Weatherwise*, April 1988.

Lindsay, John F., et al. "Sound-Producing Dune and Beach Sands." *Geological Society of America*, March 1976.

Link, Marion Clayton. "Exploring the Drowned City of Port Royal." *National Geographic*, February 1960.

Lockridge, Patricia A. "Ships, Shores & Tsunamis." *Mariners Weather Log*, September 1988.

Lynch, David K. "Tidal Bores." *Scientific American*, October 1982.

MacClary, John Stewart. "Perpetual Ice under Lava." *Natural History*, June 1936.

Malahoff, Alexander. "Hydrothermal Vents and Polymetallic Sulfides of the Galapagos and Gorda/Juan De Fuca Ridge Systems and of Submarine Volcanoes." *Bulletin of the Biological Society of Washington*, December 30, 1985.

Mallory, J. K. "Abnormal Waves off the South-East Coast of South Africa." *Marine Observer*, January 1984.

Maxwell, Ted A., and C. Vance Haynes, Jr. "Large-Scale, Low-Amplitude Bedforms (Chevrons) in the Selima Sand Sheet, Egypt." *Science*, March 3, 1989.

Meaden, G. T.:
"Circle Formation in a Wiltshire Cereal Crop—An Eye-Witness Account." *Journal of Meteorology*, 1989, Vol. 14, p. 265.
"The Formation of Circular-Symmetric Crop-

Damage Patterns by Atmospheric Vortices." *Weather*, January 1989.

"Giant Hail Causes Air Crash." *Journal of Meteorology*, May 1977.

" 'Meteor' Hits House, Sears Man's Hand." *Palo Alto Times*, January 24, 1955.

"Meteorite Comes through Roof." *Boston Globe*, November 10, 1982.

Monastersky, Richard. "Cameroon Clouds: Soda Source?" *Science News*, June 20, 1987.

Mooney, Michael J. "Malstrøm—The Legend and the Reality." *Mariners Weather Log*, January, February, March 1989.

Mullen, Daniel P. "Forecasting for the Frigid Desert of Antarctica." *Weatherwise*, December 1987.

Muraca, Gary. "Archbald Pothole Reaches Milestone." *Scranton Times*, October 28, 1984.

Murphy, Cullen. "Notes: Earth Cookie." *Atlantic*, April 1985.

"The Mystery of the Wheat Spinners." *Wall Street Journal*, September 22, 1989.

Neal, A. B., I. J. Butterworth, and K. M. Murphy. "The Morning Glory." *Weather*, May 1977.

"Niagara Roar Almost Stilled Back in 1848." *Buffalo Courier-Express*, March 29, 1955.

Nicholson, Thomas D. "The Northern Lights Head South." *Natural History*, November 1989.

O'Keefe, John A. "The Tektite Problem." *Scientific American*, August 1978.

Pachur, H. J., and S. Kröpelin. "Wadi Howar: Paleoclimatic Evidence from an Extinct River Sytem in the Southeastern Sahara." *Science*, July 17, 1987.

Palmer, Frederic. "Unusual Rainbows." *American Journal of Physics*, 1945, Vol. 13, p. 203.

"Peculiar Hailstones." *Nature*, July 13, 1893.

Petrie, Francis:
"Eerie Sound of Silence: The Day the Falls Ran Dry . . . Nearly Like Walking on Water." *Niagara Falls Review*, March 29, 1978.
"March 29, 1848: The Day the Falls Fell Silent and Troopers Rode the Brink." *Niagara Falls Review*, March 28, 1983.

Phillips, David. "The Day Niagara Falls Ran Dry." *Canadian Geographic*, April-May 1989.

"A Rare Phenomenon Moves Earth: A Huge Piece of Ground Is Mysteriously Lifted." *Philadelphia Inquirer*, November 25, 1984.

"Red Ball of Lightning in Staffordshire." *Journal of Meteorology*, 1983, Vol. 8, p. 245.

"Rogue Waves." *Science Frontiers*, November-December 1989.

Russell, George. "Colombia's Mortal Agony." *Time*, November 25, 1985.

Sadar, Anthony J. "The Awesome Aurora: 'The Heavens Declare the Glory of God.' " *Weatherwise*, April 1987.

Sawatzky, H. L., and W. H. Lehn. "The Arctic

Mirage and the Early North Atlantic." *Science*, June 25, 1976.

Schlatter, Thomas. "Why Is Some Lightning Colored?" *Weatherwise*, 1983, Vol. 36, p. 307.

Schlee, Susan. "21° North." *Science 80*, November-December 1979.

Schriever, William. "On the Origin of the Carolina Bays." *Transactions* (publication of the American Geophysical Union), February 1951.

"Scientist Vladimir Fialkov Focuses on the Future of a Unique Natural Wonder: Crystalline Lake Baikal." *People*, April 6, 1987.

Silver, Eric. "Allah's Curse: A Deadly Wall of Water." *MacLean's*, June 10, 1985.

"Small Particles Travel Far, Hitching Ride on High Winds." *Washington Post*, December 12, 1988.

Smith, F. G. Walton. "Bermuda's Mystery Waves." *Sea Frontiers*, 1985, Vol. 31, p. 161.

"Snow Rollers in Minnesota." *Weatherwise*, October 1971.

"Sparkling Rain." *Symons's Monthly Meteorological Magazine*, December 1892.

Stager, Curt. "Silent Death from Cameroon's Killer Lake." *National Geographic*, September 1987.

"Stalking the Mid-Continent Quake." *Science News*, June 14, 1980.

Stirling, Matthew W., and David F. Cupp. "Solving the Mystery of Mexico's Great Stone Spheres." *National Geographic*, August 1969.

Stommel, Henry, and Elizabeth Stommel. "The Year without a Summer." *Scientific American*, June 1979.

Stothers, Richard. "The Great Tambora Eruption in 1815 and Its Aftermath." *Science*, June 15, 1984.

Stubbs, Peter. "The Day the Med Dried Up." *New Scientist*, June 23, 1977.

Sullivan, Walter. "New Theories Link Asteroid Impacts to Major Changes in Earth's History." *New York Times*, November 1, 1988.

Thompson, Dick. "The Greening of the U.S.S.R." *Time*, January 2, 1989.

Trefil, James. "Stop to Consider the Stones That Fall from the Sky." *Smithsonian*, September 1989.

Truby, J. David. "The Blast That Shook the World: Krakatoa Explodes." *Oceans*, March 1979.

"Twister Terror: Nature Runs Wild." *Time*, April 15, 1974.

"Visible Waves Are Viable." *Science News*, May 4, 1985.

Walker, A. S. "Deserts of China." *American Scientist*, July-August 1982.

Walker, Gladys W. "The Day the Falls Ran Dry."

Niagara Falls Evening Review, March 30, 1955.

Washburn, Mark. "The Waters Above, the Storm Below." *Sky and Telescope*, 1988, Vol. 76, p. 628.

"Waterspout: Arabian Sea." *Marine Observer*, April 1984.

"Waterspout: North Atlantic Ocean." *Marine Observer*, January 1984.

"Waterspouts: Gulf of Oman." *Marine Observer*, January 1986.

"Waterspouts: Inner Hebridean Waters." *Marine Observer*, July 1982.

"Waterspouts: Singapore Strait." *Marine Observer*, April 1985.

Weisburd, Stefi:
"Cameroon: The First Wave of Clues." *Science News*, September 20, 1986.
"Largest Melt from Lightning Strike." *Science News*, October 11, 1986.

Whitehead, John A. "Giant Ocean Cataracts." *Scientific American*, February 1989.

"Why the Rocks Ring." *Pursuit*, April 1971.

Wiley, John P., Jr. "Phenomena, Comment and Notes." *Smithsonian*, October 1983.

Wilford, John Noble. "Tiny Diamonds in Space Seen as Clue to Evolution of Stars." *New York Times*, March 3, 1987.

Williams, Hill. "Cookie Cutter? Eerie Force Uproots Big Divot." *Seattle Times*, November 23, 1984.

Wilson, R. O. McD. "Blue Flash and Orographic Cloud: South African Waters." *Marine Observer*, 1986, Vol. 56, p. 20.

Wood, Richard A. "When Lightning Strikes." *Weatherwise*, August 1988.

Wright, Charles W. "The World's Most Cruel Earthquake." *National Geographic Magazine*, April 1909.

Wrightson, R. A. "The Blizzard of '88." *Weatherwise*, December 1958.

Yegorov, Alexander. "The Lessons of Baikal." *Soviet Life*, February 1989.

Other Sources

Beck, Barry F., and William C. Sinclair. "Sinkholes in Florida: An Introduction." Report 85-86-4. Orlando: Florida Sinkhole Research Institute at the University of Central Florida, 1986.

"Death Valley." Brochure by the National Park Service, U.S. Department of the Interior. Washington, D.C.: U.S. Government Printing Office, 1988.

Dill, Robert F., Lynton S. Land, and Henry P. Schwarcz. "'Blue Hole' Stalactites: Geochronological Indicators of Holocene Sea Level Rise in the Caribbean." Unpublished manuscript, University of South Carolina and Caribbean Marine Research Center, Department

of Geology, January 4, 1990.

Fairley, T. "On the Blowing Wells, near Northallerton." Paper read before the Geological and Polytechnic Society of the West Riding of Yorkshire, 1881.

"The Famous Glacial Pothole the Largest in the World." Scranton, Pa.: Lackawanna Historical Society Archives, no date.

Greene, Linda W. "A History of Mining in Death Valley National Monument" (Vol. I of II). Historic Resource Study. Denver, Colo.: National Park Service, U.S. Department of the Interior, March 1981.

Lander, James F., and Patricia A. Lockridge. "United States Tsunamis: (including United States possessions) 1690-1988." Boulder, Colo.: National Geophysical Data Center, U.S. Department of Commerce, August 1989.

"Low-Altitude Wind Shear and Its Hazard to Aviation." Committee report. Washington, D.C.: National Academy Press, 1983.

Marx, George. "On Spiders' Web." In *Proceedings of the Entomological Society of Washington*, Vol. 2, no. 4, June 30, 1893.

National Transportation Safety Board. "Aircraft Accident Report." Report no. NTISUB/B/104-76/008. Washington, D.C.: U.S. Department of Commerce National Technical Information Service, March 12, 1976.

"Origin and History of the Famous Archbald Pot-Hole." Pamphlet, Series no. 10. Scranton, Pa.: Lackawanna Historical Society, no date.

Rona, Peter A., et al. (Eds.). "Hydrothermal Processes at Seafloor Spreading Centers." Proceedings of a NATO Advanced Research Institute, held April 5-8, 1982, at the Department of Earth Sciences of Cambridge University, England. New York: Plenum Press, 1983.

Sinclair, William C., et al. "Types, Features, and Occurrence of Sinkholes in the Karst of West-Central Florida." Water-Resources Investigations Report 85-4126. Denver, Colo.: U.S. Geological Survey, U.S. Department of the Interior, 1985.

"Tsunamis: The Great Waves." Pamphlet NOAA/PA 74027. Washington, D.C.: U.S. Government Printing Office, 1975.

Wilson, William L., and Barry F. Beck. "Evaluating Sinkhole Hazards in Mantled Karst Terrane." Reprinted from *Proceedings of Geotechnical Aspects of Karst Terrains*, GT Div/American Society of Civil Engineers, Nashville, Tenn., May 10-11, 1988.

Wright, Elwood, and Pat Kenney. "The Marfa Lights: The Enigma Lights of Marfa, an Unexplained Phenomenon." Unpublished record of observation of Marfa lights, Marfa, Texas, March 14-June 16, 1973.

Index

Numbers in italics indicate an illustration of the subject indicated.

Time-Life Books Inc.
is a wholly owned subsidiary of
THE TIME INC. BOOK COMPANY

President and Chief Executive Officer:
Kelso F. Sutton
President, Time Inc. Books Direct:
Christopher T. Linen

TIME-LIFE BOOKS INC.

EDITOR: George Constable
Director of Design: Louis Klein
Director of Editorial Resources: Phyllis K. Wise
Director of Photography and Research:
John Conrad Weiser

PRESIDENT: John M. Fahey, Jr.
Senior Vice Presidents: Robert M. DeSena,
Paul R. Stewart, Curtis G. Viebranz, Joseph J. Ward
Vice Presidents: Stephen L. Bair, Bonita L.
Boezeman, Mary P. Donohoe, Stephen L. Goldstein,
Juanita T. James, Andrew P. Kaplan, Trevor Lunn,
Susan J. Maruyama, Robert H. Smith
New Product Development: Trevor Lunn,
Donia Ann Steele
Supervisor of Quality Control: James King

PUBLISHER: Joseph J. Ward

Editorial Operations
Production: Celia Beattie
Library: Louise D. Forstall
Computer Composition: Gordon E. Buck
(Manager), Deborah G. Tait, Monika D. Thayer,
Janet Barnes Syring, Lillian Daniels

**Library of Congress
Cataloging in Publication Data**
Forces of nature / by the editors of Time-Life Books.
p.   cm.   (Library of curious and unusual facts).
Bibliography: p.
Includes index.
ISBN 0-8094-7683-5
ISBN 0-8094-7684-3 (lib. bdg.)
1. Science—Miscellanea.
2. Nature—Miscellanea.
I. Time-Life Books. II. Series.
Q173.F65 1990
550—dc20   90-34046 CIP

LIBRARY OF CURIOUS AND UNUSUAL FACTS

SERIES DIRECTOR: Russell B. Adams, Jr.
Series Administrator: Elise Dawn Ritter-Clough
Designer: Susan K. White
Associate Editor: Sally Collins (pictures)

Editorial Staff for
Forces of Nature
Text Editors: John R. Sullivan (principal),
Dale Brown
Researchers: Roxie France-Nuriddin (principal),
Sydney J. Baily, M. Tucker Jones, Debra Diamond
Smit, Susan Stuck
Assistant Designer: Alan Pitts
Copy Coordinators: Jarelle S. Stein (principal),
Anne Farr
Picture Coordinator: Leanne G. Miller
Editorial Assistant: Terry Ann Paredes

Special Contributors: Lesley Coleman (London
research); Sarah Brash, Jessica Harris, Steve
Knickmeyer, Lydia Preston, Sandra Salmans (text);
Rebecca Catey, Catherine B. Hackett, Kathryn
Pfeifer, Norma Shaw (research); Hazel Blumberg-
McKee (index)

Correspondents: Elisabeth Kraemer-Singh (Bonn),
Christina Lieberman (New York), Maria Vincenza
Aloisi (Paris), Ann Natanson (Rome).
Valuable assistance was also provided by Angie
Lemmer (Bonn); Robert Kroon (Geneva); Marlin
Levin (Jerusalem); Peter Hawthorne (Johannesburg);
Elizabeth Brown (New York); Dag Christensen (Oslo);
Ann Wise (Rome); Mary Johnson (Stockholm); Dick
Berry, Mieko Ikeda (Tokyo); Traudl Lessing (Vienna).

The Consultants:
Colin Bull, Professor Emeritus of Geology and Min-
eralogy at Ohio State University, has studied glaciers in the Arctic and led numerous expeditions to
the Antarctic Peninsula and to the ice-free areas of
Victoria Land, where Bull Pass and Bull Lake are
named for him.

Clark R. Chapman, a senior scientist with the Plan-
etary Science Institute, Science Applications International in Arizona, specializes in the physical studies of small bodies in the Solar System, including
asteroids, comets, and meteoroids.

William R. Corliss, the general consultant for the
series, is a physicist-turned-writer who has spent the
last twenty-five years compiling collections of
anomalies in the fields of geophysics, geology, ar-
chaeology, astronomy, biology, and psychology.

Alistair B. Fraser, a professor of meteorology at the
Pennsylvania State University, is coauthor of a textbook entitled *The Atmosphere,* as well as author of
articles in *Scientific American* and *Smithsonian.*

Calvino Gasparini, of the Istituto Nazionale di Ge-
ofisica in Rome, is a seismologist specializing in
the focal mechanisms and surface effects of Mediterranean earthquakes.

Robert Giegengack, a professor of geology at the
University of Pennsylvania, specializes in the history
of climatic change, with particular attention to the
development of techniques that permit assigning
ages to geologic events.

David M. Ludlum, editor of WEATHERWISE magazine
from 1948 to 1978, is a weather historian who is
currently engaged in writing books and magazine
articles.

Fred Schaaf is the author of *Wonders of the Sky,
The Starry Room,* and meteorological articles in
Sky and Telescope. He has written a weekly newspaper column about astronomical events for the past
fourteen years.

Marcello Truzzi, a professor of sociology at Eastern
Michigan University, is also director of the Center
for Scientific Anomalies Research (CSAR) and editor
of its journal, *Zetetic Scholar.*

Other Publications:

AMERICAN COUNTRY
VOYAGE THROUGH THE UNIVERSE
THE THIRD REICH
THE TIME-LIFE GARDENER'S GUIDE
MYSTERIES OF THE UNKNOWN
TIME FRAME
FIX IT YOURSELF
FITNESS, HEALTH & NUTRITION
SUCCESSFUL PARENTING
HEALTHY HOME COOKING
UNDERSTANDING COMPUTERS
LIBRARY OF NATIONS
THE ENCHANTED WORLD
THE KODAK LIBRARY OF CREATIVE PHOTOGRAPHY
GREAT MEALS IN MINUTES
THE CIVIL WAR
PLANET EARTH
COLLECTOR'S LIBRARY OF THE CIVIL WAR
THE EPIC OF FLIGHT
THE GOOD COOK
WORLD WAR II
HOME REPAIR AND IMPROVEMENT
THE OLD WEST

*For information on and a full description of any of
the Time-Life Books series listed above, please call
1-800-621-7026 or write:*
Reader Information
Time-Life Customer Service
P.O. Box C-32068
Richmond, Virginia 23261-2068

This volume is one in a series that explores
astounding but surprisingly true events in history,
science, nature, and human conduct. Other books in
the series include:

*Feats and Wisdom of the Ancients
Mysteries of the Human Body*

Time-Life Books Inc. offers a wide range of fine re-
cordings, including a *Rock 'n' Roll Era* series. For
subscription information, call 1-800-621-7026 or
write Time-Life Music, P.O. Box C-32068, Richmond,
Virginia 23261-2068.